When Memories
Nudge You Softly

Also by John P. Gawlak

A Voice in the Village Square

When Memories Nudge You Softly

A Compilation of Articles Written for the Witherell Times

John P. Gawlak

iUniverse, Inc.
Bloomington

When Memories Nudge You Softly
A Compilation of Articles Written for the Witherell Times

Cover Art: John Cubeta
Production Assistance: Carol Gawlak, Jennie Gawlak, Mary Bruce, June Brice and Charles Gawlak

iUniverse books may be ordered through booksellers or by contacting:

iUniverse
1663 Liberty Drive
Bloomington, IN 47403
www.iuniverse.com
1-800-Authors (1-800-288-4677)

ISBN: 978-1-4620-1137-7 (sc)
ISBN: 978-1-4620-1138-4 (ebk)

Printed in the United States of America

iUniverse rev. date: 05/17/2011

For My Family

My Wife – Carol

My Daughter – Catharine Hope: her husband Vincent Anthony Paradiso: their children: Michael Vincent, Nicholas Arthur and Jennifer Catharine

My Sons –

Peter John (Casey); his wife Jennie; and their children: Joseph Peter, Jeffrey Charles and Annelise Jean

Thomas Stanley (Smokey); his wife Patricia; and their children: Brian Thomas and William John

Charles Andrew; and his wife Kimberly; and their children: Olivia Hope, Natalie Marie, Charles Downs and Emily Rose

<u>And the Cats</u>

Sebastian, Sushi, Blu, Trix, Indy, Buster and Brainy

Gone Home: Homer, Barney, Priscilla, Bill, Rocky, Matthew, Savannah and Higgins

Contents

Remembrance

Meaningful Memories That Endear and Endure

Trapped in their confinement, burdened by infirmity, isolated from family and friends, it is a doleful place with no escape. So I open the window of fleeting freedom. To provide momentarily, tendrils of Youth and Love and Happiness. To gently squeeze their hearts, lift their spirits and bring the warmth of a smile. I take them back on Gossamer Wings and for a moment, I stir their memories and make them young again. I bring a Ray of Sun, the blossom of flowers, the song of birds, and the rhyme of the poet inside their rooms.

Reverie

I would ask of you my Darling,
A question soft and low,
That gives me many a heartache
As the moments come and go.
When my hair shall shade the snowdrifts,
And mine eyes shall dimmer grow,
I would lean upon some loved one,
Through the valley as I go.
I would claim of you a promise,
Worth to me a world of gold,
It is only this my darling,
That you'll love me when I'm old

Author Unknown

I am fair and young,
But the rose may fade,
From my soft young cheek one day:
Will you love me then,
Mid the falling leaves,
As you did 'mong the blossoms of May?

A Woman's Question by Lena Lathrop

When Memories Nudge You Softly

Come Find Yourself

"Whatever we lost, like a you or a me, it is always ourselves we find in the sea", writes e. e. cummings. It is early summer, and a cool breeze invigorates your thoughts as you walk along the shore. In sheltered places, the sun warms your memories and you smile. Come sit alone … free your mind of everyday busy pretenses … look out over the horizon, and let the ripples of the surf draw out hidden truths that you've submerged for so long. Questions you must ask yourself to find out if you have been true to the call … are bonded in layers of substance. Are you really what you promised yourself to be … did you follow the plan … complete the blueprint … traversed the path you devised for yourself so long ago? Or have the compromises that you made turned out a less than hoped for ideal? Sometimes it is hard to accept that some of the luster of your innocence is forever lost. At our age we have no need to pursue the future … those endeavors belong to our children and grandchildren. The present, today, isn't that enough? Isn't it sufficiently difficult to win the day? And you try to retrieve the dreams that have dissipated … but the ache in your heart won't let you cover the false patches you pretend are not there. At night when the stars come out and match the beauty of the boundless sea, you try to pick out the star that bears your name … but it twinkles a message you alone can understand. It is never too late to start over … to climb that hill that holds that view you painted for yourself so long ago. It is there if you want it. In the meantime only you know your hidden heart … but that counterfeit look in your eyes gives you away … and the sea cries for you. Don't let your promises of long ago turn into forlorn fantasies … come sit by the sea and find yourself … the magic will surprise you … and you will become young once more and laugh again.

Homer – That Darned Old Cat

We had a cat named Homer. We get pensive when we think about him. Gee!!! We loved that "darned old cat". You would have loved him too, had you met him. Homer was your ordinary gray-black tabby. His fur was soft, his eyes mischievous, and he carried his tail in a special manner. He was distinguished by extra-ordinary white markings, especially around his paws. The kids decided that it was time for a pet. In the middle of winter I came home one evening with Homer tucked inside my coat. The kids shrieked with delight when they saw his tiny face emerge between the buttons. Thus began a love affair that goes on still. That cat never walked his first year. He was so cute we all took turns holding him for long periods. And he loved to sleep in your lap with his feet in the air. Nobody carried Homer more than our daughter. That cat seemed to be a part of her. But I don't think Homer appreciated being dressed as a doll. He sure loved to play with string. If you didn't watch him closely, you would end up pulling yards of string out of his stomach. As he grew older and ventured outside, he would catch and bring home, birds, moles, mice, and baby squirrels and rabbits. He never bothered skunks. He knew better. Homer loved to sleep on our beds. When he wanted to go out early in the morning he had a ritual. First he would nuzzle close to your ear and purr as loud as he could. If you ignored that, he would walk hastily up and down your body. When that failed he would climb on the headboard and jump heavily on your back. As a last resort he would stick his paw in your nostril and rake. Try ignoring that. When Carol would cook a chicken or a turkey, he never left the kitchen. When we went away for a few days, we left him behind with a neighbor. When we returned he would let you know how upset he had been. And for a month, he would never leave you out of his sight. Gosh he loved ham. He would sit by your chair and beg for pieces. One evening I was eating late and had to leave the table for a moment. When I returned, the ham was gone. Licking himself in the corner was Homer. He was funniest when he chased his tail. He was most somber looking out the window on a rainy day. He was good at breaking up fights among other cats. He would charge between them with a low scowl and the combatants would drift away. At Christmas

4

he would be the first to open his gift. While we were asleep, he would somehow find his present and tear it to shreds to get at his toy mouse filled with catnip. When we came down in the morning, paper was scattered everywhere, and the decorations and tinsel were stripped from the lower part of the tree. One day Homer became sick and we took him to the vet. Diagnosis: lung cancer. He became less active and spent most of his time sleeping in the sun. One day he went to sleep under the dining room table, and did not eat or drink for three days. We knew it was time to send Homer to that city of golden litter boxes where all good cats go. We all cried and were downcast for days. After a while we got another gray-black tabby and named him Barney. He is a loveable thing but there will never be another Homer, that "darned old cat".

Love Calls Us On St. Valentines Day

I wish every day were Valentines Day. I wish it would last forever. Everyone seems to change on Valentines Day ... we become friendlier ... more inclined to show good will. I wish the spirit of Valentines Day would continue all year. Love and cheer would fill our days ... the dissonant voices would be stilled. The restless searching of the human heart, that we carry with the tide of human occurrences, would generate the generosity, the wonder ... the wings of gladness ... the peace within ourselves, and between each other. You see, we make holy what we believe, just as we make beautiful what we love. There are demands that love makes on all of us. It is then that we encounter opportunities to go beyond ourselves ... to explore the depth to which human emotion resounds. Do you know that the conduct of our lives is the mirror of our doctrine? It is human to want rewards and recognition ... but if they don't happen, love is enough. People, who take a venal approach to civility, diminish us all ... and if you keep hugging a lie, you will never be free. When it comes to love, we mortals can be such fools ... because love can be so simple, yet so hard for us to learn. And if you keep your love a secret, it will never multiply. If you want to keep the joy of Valentines Day ongoing, heed the song Johnny Mathis sings: "You ask how much I love you, I'll tell you true ... I'll love you 'til the 12th of never, and that's a long, long time." While time still favors, tell yours true this humble phrase, "I love you".

You Can Feel the Signs of Spring

Winter does not die easily. Dawn's first rays still have difficulty pushing away the darkness. The ground is not fully thawed. Ice is retreating from the ponds. The wind can be cutting, but the early morning chill is less numbing. The sun rises earlier and sets later, allowing longer periods of daylight. Midday seems brighter and affords a little more comfort. The birds seem more cheerful, the lawn less brown, and we ourselves seem less antagonistic toward each other. The cold indifference of early spring, in deference to the warmth to come, tries to discourage the flowers from rising. But on a cool, sunny day in March, the first crocus, like a snapping turtle in a pond, cautiously nudges its nose to the surface, and finding it safe, emerges fully to display its wardrobe. Others soon follow and lay a carpet of purple, white, yellow, orange, blue and pink. But I look beyond tomorrow and see spring in full bloom. Although early flowers cannot speak, their outward declaration of beauty, warmth, and grandeur fill volumes in people's souls. This resplendent time, like love, lives on hope and nurtures itself on friendship and caring.

Can you picture that first real warm day? When you lift your face to the sun and your spirit soars? The warmth goes deep and ignites the fire of affection. And a hidden chamber in your heart is unlocked, and releases the young dream of first love you thought abandoned. Did you know that spring submits to the arbitration of time? We do not have that privilege, but do not let that discourage you from constantly celebrating the honest fondness of nature. For it is a time to be made new, to be resurrected. A time to nourish your soul, stir your spirit, and energize your capacity for loving. Just as trees bud and flowers bloom anew, all of us must strive for a new dedication in ourselves and how we relate to each other. How close are we to real spring? If you put your ear to the ground, you will hear the flowers stirring.

By the Sea in Early Summer

The sea beckons … it offers solace and succor from a long, harsh, winter … it soothes a heart in need … you find freedom from thoughts that bind. A warm sun massages your shoulders … and the vast, calm, blue-tinged waters bring on a pleasant sigh of surrender. The cool sand under your feet relays a message of comfort … you feel at home … and wonder why you ever left. The chatter of seagulls welcomes you back … back to a place whose memories make you smile. You exchange kindred greetings with a murmuring surf. It is the distant horizon that holds your attention … and you see a place and time when love came easy. And you snare a portion of happiness … that wayward and elusive scamp we all spend our whole life pursuing. The hidden door of childhood dreams opens. Blue skies match the eyes of that girl in the third grade … and if you stand quietly and listen … you will hear her call your name … and her laughter trails off with the wind. You will always come back here. Because it is here that you pick out the patches of your life that tug at your heart. You turn the pages … out rise the hopes and dreams and wishes … the best of times … the shiniest moments. It was long ago but they are still here … you reach out and touch them … and they touch you back. When shadows of evening steal across the sky, I invite the memories to dance with my dreams. How pleasant it was to be young and innocent. But the war came along and your childhood disintegrated. Here by the sea you can remain the child you once were … and never, ever, ever have to grow up.

Drifting

Let me drift into that gossamer world where sages, prophets, and Lady Wisdom make their declarations. We are guided by the sound counsel they offer, and often recite their terse offerings. But you see there are implications beyond the moment … deeper and more profound than our daily duty … for we all fall short unless we seek a measure of eternity. Too many of us drift to the margins of life … basic assumptions become untenable … and the good we are capable of doing is lost in false smiles and plastic courtesies. It is easy to lose our bearings … but when we do, we need "cognitive reinforcement". We need to unmask the pretense and posture we have assumed … we need to go to the hilltop more often … to make room for more compassion … to manifest the tangible spirit of care and generosity … and reclaim the loving ways that touch the heart of others. When was the last time that you shared weakness without judgment or condemnation? Do you know that love is the dearest kind of relationship … and the echo of a kiss lasts forever? Never, ever, ever, become part of that contrived benevolence … that you fail to show those small acts of kindness that takes the gloom away … for if you do, you cheat yourself of life's rewards … and make yourself a fool.

An Early Fall Vacation at the Beach

The car was packed, and we smiled as we headed for our favorite New England beach. We knew the summer multitudes would be gone, and peace and serenity awaited us. The weather promised sunny and warm, with no forecast of rain. After a few hours of traveling, the scent of sea air, and a cooling breeze told us we were nearing our destination. Unpacked, we stroll to our porch, and overlook a vast and sparkling ocean that delights our senses. Yet, we know the best is yet to come. The late afternoon sun is inviting. Lounging at water's edge, we are enveloped in a warm glow that subtracts the midsummer sting. Later, a walk along the beach is in order. It is these walks that we remember most. Disturbed only by the crashing surf and the screech of seagulls, we watch sand plovers dance as they race to flee the incoming waves. Add to that the honking of wild geese as they fly in formation to their feeding grounds, and the rustle and whistling wings of wild ducks as they dodge and skim the waves. We stop and observe the baleful cry of a lonesome osprey as he circles the sky in search of prey. We continue on along the sand made smooth and firm by the never ending rush of the sea. We watch, fascinated, as schools of large bluefish, in a frenzy, pursue bunker into shallow water. After a delicious dinner, we sit on our porch amid the multi-shades of the setting sun, which beckons the sea to be still. A light jacket is needed, as a chill permeates the early evening. The moon rises and sprinkles silver everywhere. Stars are set like gems in the darkening sky. In the distance, the oscillating lighthouses tell us this day is done. We slumber to the roar of the surf, and the murmur of the foam, and dream of many tomorrows like today. Tomorrow comes, and as the early morning mist is cleared away by the unrelenting sun, the dance of yesterday begins again. The week over, there is a sadness as we head home, but inside, an efficacious tingle stirs, knowing that we will come back again and again.

Inner Strength

Inner strength manifests itself in unflagging character, unwavering adherence to principle, and unswerving moral fortitude. Like a golden thread, it weaves the sinew by which we are judged. People of inner strength are full of winning virtues ... they are distinguished by strong stands when tested ... they stand out amongst us like beacons. You see the call to character comes from within, not from above. There is a difference between having a character flaw and being devoid of character ... the former can be overcome by the individual ... the latter overcomes the individual. It prefixes their deficiency ... it reflects an inner ugliness, and carries a pernicious effect. How often have you seen corrupt officials become born again Christians when sent to prison? Or military cowards profess heroism under fire? It seems religion and patriotism becomes the last refuge of scoundrels. How many people do you know who confess to little faults to persuade themselves that they have no great ones? If we had no faults of our own, we would not take so much pleasure in noticing those of others. In Charles Dickens' classic novel, David Copperfield, development of inner strength is one of his themes. David experiences many trials ... and at one of his most painful ... at the burial sight of his mother ... his girlfriend consoles him with, "David, for steel to be true it must pass through the fire". You see character is forged by how you respond to adversity. And once molded, it remains constant, steadfast, unshakeable ... it can never be sullied by greed, selfishness, or corruption. The steady application of morality in your public and private life makes one a role model ... and leads to honorable recognition. You see, what you have means nothing ... what you are means everything.

How Do You Rate Yourself?

As the old year ends and the New Year begins, look back, and rate yourself. What grade do you deserve? What mark do you give yourself, as it applies to the redeeming merits that are expected of all of us? Has this past year of your life been signaled by integrity which is the hallmark of a just person? Or do you feel the guilt of your flawed choices? When we seem trapped by the happenings of our history, we need to be set free. But how do we do this? You see we need assurances that the constant choices we make are the right ones. It is presumed that age has a certain wisdom denied the young. If you believe that, then you possess the synergism of a bountiful journey for the New Year. Just as it is our duty to speak up to those abusing power, it is our equal duty to speak in kindness and compassion to the weak, the sick and the poor. Do you know that kindness has a rhythm … and to tear the fabric of that kindness is to bring on pain, sorrow, and suffering? Everyday, in some kind way, we must strive to lift the heart of others … to brighten a weary day … to dispel a frown … to soften anxiety … with gentle voice and soothing touch. It is not enough to fulfill the minimum conditions of decency. We all must go beyond - urged on bearing a foundation upon which all virtues are constructed. We must forget old failures and concentrate on new beginnings. Give me a wish we cry … ever asking for strength to do great things. But I find it nobler to do small things graciously. You see you can fool others, but you can never fool yourself. Be true when grading yourself … lest you find you are betrayed by what is false within … and the peace you seek will elude you, again.

A Foggy Day at the Beach

It is a strange sight to see our favorite beach enveloped in a thick fog - a mist so heavy you feel you are watching one of those scary mystery movies in foggy London come to life. The veiled creepiness makes you shiver. Everything is obscure. There are no people, no birds, no boats, and no life at all. The thundering surf, that you can barely see, appears angry and menacing. It makes the ground quiver as it crashes heavily, and adds to the eeriness. The mournful dirge of a foghorn wails on and on. You see we all fear the unknown - that which we cannot see, cannot discern. Your eyes try to pierce the web-like haze, which fills you with a haunting presence. You are left with an ominous projection of a lurking evil, danger, tragedy. You conjure thoughts of drowning in the eye of Dracula, or escaping the tentacles of a giant spider. After a while a pale glimmer of sun breaks through. Ghost-like, the first people appear ... vague images, shadowy figures. They seem like an apparition ... not real, translucent, emitting vapors. Then the first seagull flies by ... so low that his wings fan your face. It is a macabre world of shrouded gloom, and you feel uneasy. But close your eyes and sweep away the pliable portentousness. In vision, you see the sparkling merriment that a sun splashed scene can bring. The warm rays embrace you and seep into the recesses of recall. And the bursting bubbles of your youthful banter arises, making all of life's good qualities erupt like kernels of popcorn. Suddenly the sun explodes like an avenging flare, and the fog retreats and surrenders. Out of the crevasses, all forms of life come into view, and the merry-go-round of "fun at the beach" resumes. You see we all succumb to the siren song of the sun. There is advantage in wisdom won from pain. It is a lesson that no matter how desperate things seem at times, hope, goodness, and elation prevail. You can rest in the assurance that tomorrow will be better. Do not live among the shadows. Lift your face and feel the sunlight.

Choices

You and I are the products of many choices, rendered by many people in our lives - choices made by our parents, teachers, instructors, mentors, counselors, and all others who had a share in our education and maturation. Emerson writes, "As a man thinketh so he is: as a man chooseth so is he." You see we are all compelled by conviction. When we finish the framework that forms the matrix of our matter, our mind, our manners, our mores and merits, all of us make choices we call, "doing the right thing". These choices lead us to be: cruel or kind; greedy or generous; affable or arrogant; magnanimous or mendacious; sensitive or sarcastic; vivacious or vindictive; humiliating or humble; invidious or inviting; honorable or hateful; forgiving or furtive. The ability to make good choices in our lives are handsome gifts indeed that fate and nature lend us. Bad choices are sensibilities that appeal to the vulgar. To the mean eye all things are trivial. Evil looms as part of our daily life and confronts us with choices. But I would admonish you, never, ever, ever, ever become part of that depravity that springs from choices that paralyze your senses, brutalize your soul, and mutilate your spirit. You will never erase the stigma and you invite eternal self-vituperation. To love is to choose those features that pierce all hearts with pleasantries. Without tenderness and affection, without love that redeems, we bruise the very ones who are closest. Never make yourself inaccessible to the imploration of others for love and understanding. Never choose to stand mute to the entreaty of others for a measure of warmth to soothe their solitude. In my penchant to counsel, my urging to you is, to be true to the covenant of kindness that binds us all to the mission of improving the human condition. In making decisions never compromise yourself. People of good will are never troubled by a bad conscience. The good choices we make stand the test of time. The bad ones haunt us until time is no more. Are you happy with the choices you have made? I am with mine.

A Snowbelle Blooms in December

Was it a warm December that caused a lone Snowbelle to blossom in my desolate garden in winter? While strolling in my backyard one day, near Christmas time, I was startled to see a lone Snowbelle in full bloom. Mind you, Snowbelles flower with the Crocuses in early Spring. While it is not profound, it does pose a riddle. What would be profound, were a butterfly to alight on that lonely blossom. I stand under that cold, muted sky of winter and recall the poets' plea: "The summer flowers have gone to sleep … the smiling of Autumn weeps…" I study the phenomena of that exquisite little white blossom … and I want to bid farewell to Winter's wrath, and touch the face of Spring. But it is only December, and the Ides of March are distant. Do you know that crystal stars that sparkle in a wintry evening bring the promises of tomorrow? I have been taught to enjoy the simple things in life: walk barefoot on cool, moist sand … feel the morning dew on soft, green grass … hear the far-off skylark sing … leave your footprints on new fallen snow … and now I have found another: A lonely Snowbelle nods in December, and fills you with a secret mirth. Perhaps the riddle may be the soul that has no established aim, loses itself. James Whitcomb Riley says it better: "Tis love forever smiling, fragrant retrospection from the blossoms in my heart." If you hunger after treasure, let it be the lasting kind … like finding a lone Snowbelle blooming in December.

Thank Heaven for Little Girls

We are all enchanted by the innocent wonder of babies. They bring the morning . . . new and born and fresh and wonderful. And when Maurice Chevalier sings, "Thank Heaven for Little Girls … for little girls get bigger every day" … the spirit within her whispers softly and she scatters rainbows. Our first granddaughter, Jennifer Catharine, was born July 1st. When you hold her for the first time, she radiates that indefinable aura … you invoke that ancient injunction that babies everywhere mystify and captivate … those little hands and feet … but it is the eyes that "send you crashing through the ceiling". And I cull from the rhyme of the poet these tender verses that put the dance to poetry and violins to love: she forms an airy grace delicate and silky … she is love forever smiling … her sighs are the drowsy hum of crickets reaching across the edge of sleep … her sleepy face radiates the warm glow of the sun and the blush of sunset … her azure eyes as tender as the sky. It is always time to cuddle little ones … I feel the squeeze of her tiny little fingers and I ask how can I fashion the dream in her heart? The whisp of wind in the babe's first cry gives me reason to sing, "Hush my child for I am here." The tiny scarlet ribbon in her hair manifests the beauty of butterflies … comfort and peace in her sleepy eyes. We wish great things for this little babe … joy and peace and hope and happiness. I imagine when she grows up she most certainly will hear that old sailors pitch, "Was your mother a thief? Then who stole the stars and placed them in your eyes?" She will be christened in a few weeks, and will be blessed with that special spiritual exhortation: "Those marked with the sign of the cross, go boldly into the night."

Christmas Journey

Christmas is the time to make that inner journey ... to respond to the call we all receive to come home ... home where we all become children again ... innocent, playful, loving, pensive. That time to sit quietly on Christmas Eve and listen to the spiritual side of yourself ... that peaceful, serene, uninterrupted, placid center of ourselves that calls to us ... that makes us guard against the power of darkness. To drowsily immerse ourselves in the nobility of grace ... grace that is not submissive to the ravages of time, rancor, impudence, guile. Grace that soars in its uniqueness and illuminates all who are attracted to it ... touched by it ... befriended with it. We are challenged by the personal demons in our lives everyday ... but you see, what matters most is how your respond. Christmas is a time of giving ... so give of your substance, not your surplus. Do not promise according to your hopes then perform according to your fears. Make a Christmas promise to pursue a course less self-serving ... and more noble and pure in purpose. Avoid that life of pious fraud which comes from betrayal by what is false within. For too many of us, we prefer to spend our days wandering in small comfortable circles through the routine of our lives. Christmas is that time ... that summons ... to get off the carousel and start up the mountain ... to follow the "Star of Wonder" that beckons us to the mountaintop ... to look past the present ... to look beyond the horizon of eternity. My wish for all of you is to be happy with that sacred peace on Christmas day.

Happiness

Happiness is as difficult to define as it is to achieve. Yet it is the one most singular possession we all diligently pursue. There are many misconceptions about happiness. Some claim it lies in professional accomplishment, financial gain, material acquisition, power, fame, or social station. To me it is none of these. They are all impostors. They steal from you the insights and energies necessary in fulfilling the search for the true treasure. There is an unwritten directive that states, "If you are to find happiness, you must first make those around you happy." And Byron writes, "All who would win joy must share it. Happiness was born a twin." The ingredients of happiness are qualities that enrich: honesty, integrity, character, sincerity, tradition, and principle. Of these are born inner peace, serenity, and comfort of the soul. These are themes of all good love stories, poetry, love songs, music, and the simplistic appreciation of the inherent and abundant beauty in nature. This is the unselfish manifestation of the goodness that flows from those who give freely of themselves to others. The disparity in all of us is our inability to recognize values that pull us asunder. Michael Douglas in the movie, "Wall Street", addresses a group of stockholders and says, "Greed is good". And when he finishes his explanation, everyone believes him. But the truth is, greed suffocates happiness. You see happiness is found outside of ourselves. We are called to that covenant of kindness, caring, compassion, that commands all of us to extend a venerate hand to the afflicted, the lonely, the fragile, the forgotten – to the weary and to the wounded, especially to the broken who are marked by the hardship of the human condition. You measure your happiness by the hearts you have softened. Make gentleness and warmth the mothers' milk of your daily actions. I read somewhere that happiness is like a butterfly, the more you chase it, the more it will elude you. But if you turn your attention to other things, it comes and softly sits on your shoulder.

Spring – The Greening of Our Soul

Spring is a time to contemplate the opening flower … that manifests the creation power … the promise of tomorrow. Daffodils and tulips tolerate the cool weather … but nothing foments thoughts of Spring more than when lilacs, dogwoods, and azaleas are in full bloom. Enjoy the richness of Spring's glory … the verdancy mitigates the malice of others … when the gentle sun bathes your face in warmth … and we probe that nostalgic, dream-filled time when we were young … when love and affection flowed freely. If flowers had a soul, do you wonder where they would go? I surmise that they would go to that place beneath the volcano, where all good souls go … and when evil is perpetrated anywhere in the world, the good souls stir and the earth trembles. Spring fills us with the unassailable need to do the right thing … to take pleasure in the triumph of a good person … to constantly be inquisitive to the truth … to seek the noble soul that lights the flame of love … to sprinkle the stardust that uplifts the self-esteem and dignity of others. In the cool, bright, starry evening, we are inspired to kindle the moon … run with the wind … use the clouds for your pillow … echo the voices of waterfalls. In the quiet sanctuary of your soul, you open the chest of your most treasured moments and scan the scroll … drifting by are the names, the faces, the events, the memories that keep your heart warm and your soul smiling. Ah!! Spring!! The quiet and peaceful time in our lives … a time to rest your spirit in her solitary haven … a time to ride the gossamer wings of a humming bird and seek the nectar of life.

A Tribute to St. Valentine

Valentines Day is a special day when you express your love … a day when you are not afraid to show your softer, warmer side. You express your fondness for those very dear to you. It is a day of your greatest happiness. Happiness is that inner glow that warms your heart … and comes only from loving and being loved in return. The spirit of love associated with Valentines Day does not respond to hesitant stirrings … because it is bold … and true … and amplified. St. Valentine says: "Be not a stern, cruel judge of others even in your injured dignity … love bears no ill will. Fill yourself with an abundance of love and share it with everyone." Do you know that one of life's greatest sins is to withhold love … to deny others that supreme emotion? Andrew Greeley writes: "Love is the passionate and devout commitment of one person to the welfare and happiness of another. Love is a fundamental longing of humankind … a basic aspiration of human nature … but suspicion and distrust kill it for many of us." We mortals are such fools … for we often exact a price for our liberation. True friends, true lovers, are concerned about the other in a way we normally reserve for ourselves. And despite the emotional intensity of such love and friendship, we do not grow weary from it. You keep the fires of love burning not by thinking of yourself, but by being concerned with the good of the other. Not in getting, but in giving, lies the secret of it all. If you want to experience that mystic interlude … be generous with self-giving affection. May your Valentines Day be lovely.

Spring into Summer

Every year we all await the arrival of spring, which can be full of surprises. Sometimes its arrival is late and brief, plunging right into summer. This year Spring hedged but when she finally arrived, we forgave her duplicity. How fresh and green the landscape ... daffodils and tulips a magnificent array of fragile colors ... azaleas and dogwoods vibrant displays of majesty. The warm sun penetrates your latent cynicism, and allows your winter-weary spirit to ascend and rejoice. That first warm day, the angels trumpet that ancient truth ... where blue skies brush away the gray ... and your woes are swept aside. Do you know that we are made for heaven? And spring gives us a glimpse into that land of golden enchantment? It brings on the smiles ... the twinkle to your eyes ... the song to your voice ... the healing to your touch. Spring ignites the transformation that defines our trinity of solicitous emotions ... it marks that point in time to resurrect your loving nature. It is the season that brings forth that hidden magic that empowers us to flood our days with deep feelings of love, and charity, and abiding companionship. And you sigh, "If I were king." Take time to appreciate nature's gift ... walk on the wings of spring ... seek your true self in her blend of colors. Has it ever occurred to you that to see evil, and to be unable to remedy it because of human perversity, is the greatest anguish of all? Those who do good are bound by a common spirit, for the foundation of all love and goodness is from eternity not time. When you fail to live up to the standards of goodness and decency, your culpability becomes a compelling aspect that brings your integrity into question. In whatever you do, let your motives become so transparent that no one can ever question your will to do good.

Quiet Time

Amid the clamor of our daily lives, besieged by constant demands and urgencies, we need a "quiet time" ... a daily period to absorb ourselves in the grace of the moment ... to reflect upon our life, past and present, and to develop a spiritual sense for the future. We need to be by ourselves ... to close our eyes and shut out the common interruptions and intrusions of the day ... to hear another voice calling ... to reach up and touch those memories that make you smile. We need to sit quietly and listen ... listen to the whispers beyond the stars ... to see beyond the veil of flesh and to comprehend the divine intimacy of our God. Inspired by the Gospel ethic, we need to ask ourselves, "What is our summons?" We need to resist the forces of evil. We must move away from the standard of the world to the standard of goodness. We need to love without condition for love knows no limits. Our greatest need is boundless love tempered by inner peace. We must cease to deny responsibility for the wrong we do. Give thanks for your faith and the freedom to express it. Never, ever, ever, become so busy where you fail to schedule your "quiet time". Without it you will never be free. For you see, we let very few people share our private dreams ... we allow very few to become our emotional equals. But at quiet time, you will find peace comes gently like a soft-spoken message from above. When we are unable to find tranquility within ourselves, it is useless to seek it elsewhere.

Summertime

Just let me wander with some random thoughts about the summers that were kind to me. The summers seem longer now ... they were shorter when I was young. It got cold right after Labor Day, and going back to school wrote the end to summer fun. But no matter the age, the beauty of summer is everlasting ... it holds the promise of happiness ... the flowers tell us to be open to the call of others ... to scatter, like confetti, those gems of kindness that abide in us all ... to peal the love bells in our hearts. Do you ever wonder what lies in the bosom of a rose? I believe we all fall in love too easily in summer ... with ourselves ... our families ... our jobs ... our surroundings ... that is why you must never argue with the insights of those who see only with the eyes of love. The exotic fragrance of night blooming jasmine takes me back to the river of my youth ... and the sweet / sad vulnerability of summer love ... the haunting eyes of that girl in the third grade ... the tow-headed boy running the beach on the Connecticut River ... singing a song that would never be written ... weaving a dream that would become the structure of my life ... for you see it is destiny that grants us our wishes. In the cool of evening, when you sit quietly in your yard, and dusk beckons the fireflies to begin their dance, close your eyes and you will find yourself climbing that hill to see that view that you maybe only get to see once in your life. Opportunities arise to sort out the major themes in your life ... the convictions we live by ... the wellspring of our courage and hope ... and the daily profound human need to find meaning in life. Do you know that most people never get to realize how rich they really are? It is summertime and our thoughts are easy ... but it is the "wind in the willows" that gives us pause.

Niagara Falls: Sights, Sounds, Sentiments

In the mind of what artist has this grandeur been concocted? Is it possible for mortals to synergize beauty of this magnitude? But let us not get ahead of ourselves. The ride is long and tiring. But the restful scenery, quaint farms, and miles of heather make it palatable. As we approach the city and cross the Rainbow Bridge into Canada, you get your first look at the falls. A giant cloud of mist and spray rises from the thundering waters. All quiets down, nobody speaks, because the sight is a precursor of the delight to come. We dine in a tower restaurant overlooking the falls. As darkness sets in, multi-colored lights flash forth and bathe the rumbling waters - first white, then red, blue, and orange. There is something artificial in this but the scent stirs your aesthetic sense. And the best is yet to come. The next morning we board the "Maid of the Mist" which takes us right under the falls. As we enter the abyss, the water cascades into your face. You look up and become frightened as you see the surge of 140 million gallons per minute descent to crush you. The roar is deafening. You don't move, you don't breathe, you don't think. You feel as if you are in limbo awaiting the call to heaven. You become part of the deluge that tumbles down. Emerging from the chasm, you are greeted by a rainbow miraculous in color and setting. Immersed in this emotional sciamachy, you are transformed and will never be the same again. You feel cleansed from the inundation. Your imagination out of control, in the glistening sun of the mist, the apparition of an Indian rises and dances. In his painted splendor, he seems to be saying, "this is the place of my ancestors, disturb not their sleep, profane not their spirits". As we gently pull further away the sun ripples off of the rim of the falls, 150 feet high. You then know in your heart that the goodness of the centuries gently sleeps here and all is well in this turbulent world. Sleep is difficult as I reflect the commercialization of the city. I feel tourism exacts a Caesarian measure that is unwanted and unnecessary. The carnival atmosphere disrupts the truism of the natural order and makes it apocryphal. So I ally myself with the Indian and enjoin his spirit ... and lament the age's long indiscretions. There are good things about the city. Its well-manicured parks, prodigious flowers, fruit orchards, vineyards, historical monuments, are a story unto itself. As we leave, re-crossing the Rainbow Bridge, you take your final look at the falls. As you settle back for the long ride home, you surely feel that you've been expurgated by the baptismal waters of the river Jordan.

How Pleasant to be by the Side of the Sea

What strikes you first is the immensity … a glimpse into the comprehension of eternity … endless, timeless, expansiveness. Next comes liberation from the stifling pervasiveness of the workplace. And finally the serenity … where sun, sky, sand, and sea form an emulsion … an elixir that brings a smile to your soul … and makes your heart quiver. I don't know why, but for some reason, the sea becomes calm at sundown. And when the sky reflects a pink hue, it proclaims that mariners ode: "Pink sky at night, sailors delight". When the tide is full, the surf is pristine … but when low, it becomes mixed with sand and muddled. When the last strip of daylight is lost in the western sky, the first star appears and beckons his companions to join him. Darkness now prevails and the universe becomes a gigantic pincushion imbedded with diamonds. Here I pose you a riddle: "Can you tell me the number of stars, and call them by name?" This is not intellectual arrogance … but a quiet conversation with a fellow shipmate while standing the midnight watch on a calm, starry night, in the South Pacific fifty years ago. It is late … the night filled with magic. The surf roars on reveling in its mystery. And I will dream of that time when our love was young … and we promised it would last forever and beyond … and nothing … neither time, nor circumstance, nor tribulation will ever change it. You see, all love craves unity … for love to be consummated it must pass through the fire of communion … and in the stately silence of this night; it is communion with the sea.

Bermuda

We disembark from the plane, and on the ride to the resort you are exuberant at the eye pleasing multi-shades of pastel colored houses that dot the hillside. The profuse stretch of pretty colored flowers brings thoughts of rainbows. On your terrace you scan the waters that are graded in colors of light green, aqua, columbia and royal blue, according to depth. Unlike the coarse sand of New England, you are enthralled by the pink tint of the beaches, which are smooth and as soft as silk. And when you walk at waters edge, your footprints disappear immediately. The rocks and ledges are sharp and jagged from centuries of wear by the constant pounding of the surging sea and whipping winds, as old as time yet eternally new. It is the place where the yellow bird carouses, and the chattering long tails dive and dodge with reckless abandon. The warm sun beckons you to lounge as the muted surf lulls you to sleep. Bermuda is one huge flower garden, where oleander and morning glories grow wild, and lilies blossom in bunches. And when you encounter the exotic blue African lily, you realize that the beauty of flowers everywhere carry a message. Do you know what it is? Sure you do. Flowers never manipulate, never negotiate. All they ever do is elicit an enthusiastic response to the gift of love. Being here is one of the few times in your life where you feel deserving to do nothing – to be carefree, unscheduled, unmonitored, totally and uncompromisingly free from the stifling urgency of workday tasks. To overlook the panoramic, wide screen view of whitecaps on a mosaic, shimmering sea … glimmering beaches … rustling pine and palm trees … jewel blue skies … and not feel guilty of what and whom you left behind. Here, artists, poets, authors, philosophers, germinate the seeds of artistic chimera. Creative genes come into play, and the human spirit is unbound and releases the thoughts, the phrases, the rhyme, the dictum, the story line, the profound statements, that make the populous richer indeed. You see, all great inspirations are timeless. Go see Bermuda. It is everything you have heard and more.

Late Summers Footsteps in the Sand

With summer ending, we are back at the beach we love. The crowds are gone. The sun is brittle and barely warms the sand. Down at the waters edge, the interminable surf rolls on. And as you gaze down the long empty stretch of beach, you can almost see summer leaving. Summers end at the shore is a still, untroubled retreat. You reply to the whisper of the sea in quiet voices. The green tint of the water is more vivid. The delineation of the scalloped clouds and the angel-eyed blue of the sky become so protracted that you can see beyond the horizon. The cast of feathered players are present: seagulls struggle against the wind, piping plovers race the surf as if they are afraid to get their feet wet, ducks and geese fly in migratory formation, loons dive and stay submerged for long periods, and bluefish flash in the sun as they dash near shore. Walking along the open beaches, you unburden your mind, unshackle the fetters from your heart, and release the bindings of your soul. Standing there with your feet in the sand and your head in the heavens, you are mesmerized by the vast expanse of sea and sky. In reverie, your free spirit soars, and you are yesterday's youthful, innocent scamp again. Illusory faces drift by. Fueled by imagination, you select the childhood girl of your dreams. You recall the first time you fell in love - your first clumsy kiss, the first time you held hands, the painful shyness you could never overcome. Thoughts that never leave you and forever nestle softly in your memory. You are brought back to today by the groan of a ship's whistle. You rub your arms to ward off the chill. In the twilight, faint shadows in the distance beckon you to dinner. As the sun closes the door on another day, the mural it paints fills you with a peaceful conciliation. Night comes quickly in this late season. In the clear, cool, evening, the fluorescent glow of tiny stars makes you tingle. The moon, silver fragments weaving its way from wave to wave, the music of the rhythmical surf composes its song and plays on endlessly. In this tranquility, you close your eyes and you are at peace with yourself and the world. Because safe and warm within your heart, the last vestiges of summer gently sleep.

Autumn at the Seashore

It was chilly when we arrived. Having settled in our room, we walked by waters edge. The storm had subsided and the beach was washed flat and firm. The surf was soft as if sleeping ... the rush so mild it would not awaken a slumbering child. A gentle wind nudged your face ... and if you stood still and listened, it lilted the laughter of that girl in the third grade ... riding its conveyance were the muted happy voices of the grandchildren. The sun tried to warm with a willowy touch ... like a child's light caress. The sea stood still ... no waves ... no whitecaps ... only a gentle rolling that carried your thoughts beyond the horizon. There are few people here this time of the year ... this season, when summer has taken leave and autumn enters to begin her stroll toward winter. The solitary reconditeness is a welcome from the roiling responsibility of the workplace. Pleasure craft are gone ... cottages are shuttered ... the multitudes absent ... constant reminders that only the sea prevails. There is no need to speak in this aura of peaceful splendor ... just listen and gaze in wonder ... as the gifts of nature's bounty whisper their secrets ... their longing ... their eternal message. You are captive to the sea's eternity ... the sky's infinity ... the sun's diffusion of grace ... and the soul- placating solitude. Night falls and the sky is strangely dark. A crescent moon swings low and if you jump, you can touch it. Stars, like beacons of love, are inserted in this fudge sky ... as numerous as grains of sand. With the great love of my life at my side, silence prevails ... for our eyes hold, the story untold, the mysteries of life unfold. You see, the sea offers the capital of friendship ... it is for all times and all seasons ... and we walk a common ground. I am spirit ... and mystery ... and timeless ... and abide in all.

Some Thoughts on Winter

We are beyond the half-mark of winter, and why is it that many of us seem impervious to the sublime qualities of this cold season? There are discomfort and hazards, but other seasons also have their distractions. Allow me to make trenchant commentary on the winters of our life. The cold winds cut without wounding ... your teeth chatter ... your cheeks smart ... your toes throb ... and being so trundled you look for someone to hug so that you can stay warm. And we all are afraid to be alone in winter. Early darkness ... desolate surroundings ... haunting wind ... eerie sky ... voices seem distant ... and more than at any other time, you are forced to face your heart and listen to the soft, pealing voice of your soul. It is a time when winter sweeps its rapine hand and ravages everything. And yet, to awaken to new fallen snow ... when winters ugliness is shielded ... the brightness releases the imprisoned loveliness of the ages. The dark dimension of winter's personality withers, and we extricate ourselves from this brooding, robbing, mindset. You see, you must endure the night to fully appreciate the first light of dawn. Soon the wild flowers will blossom, and the warm sun will race to your inner recesses and tingle your dormant dreams. When we brush aside the pain and the hurt, we are happiest when we recall the pleasant memories in our lives.

1994: A New Beginning

1993 has passed into history, and with it much we wish we had never been part of ... misbehavior, mistakes, impetuousness, jealousy, spitefulness, acts of vindication that we would like to submerge. We are on the threshold of 1994, and we have the opportunity to reclaim that part of ourselves ... that part of our character that stood aside while the lesser traits marched boldly to the fore ... brought our dark side to the surface ... and left us with eerie echoes of past pit-falls. You see it is by our faults and transgressions that we compromise the "new righteousness", and we fail to realize our true destiny. Look back and recall the times you used veiled assertions to cover your flaws and inadequacies ... the times you responded coldly when warmth was needed. 1994 is the time to comport yourself with that unyielding spirit when confronted with compromising situations. Vow to make a kind word, a warm smile, a gentle touch, a soothing gesture explode with promise. In your glistening eyes let others see the song of joy and peace you keep in your heart ... make others want to emulate the riches of spirit and power of divinity you display. Make a promise to lift the aching heart of others ... help the weary dream the sunny hours away ... assist the wounded find the peace they seek. Lady wisdom proclaims, "Those vested with authority must use it with respect and for service". Woe to those who abuse that dictum ... who fail to lead by example and inspiration. People who have a need ... who use their subliminal urges to make others feel inferior ... carry a vagueness in their eyes that betrays them. I believe all of us have seen too much love erased by selfishness, arrogance, pride, and inability to reconcile. The New Year is your chance to foster change ... to again find the trappings of your heritage ... to become what you promised yourself to be. Retain what is good ... avoid any semblance of evil ... let the spirit manifest itself ... let the spirit show you the way. The New Year allows us to continue the restrained drama of our lives with contextual alacrity ... how will you respond???

Far From Home

While driving upstate one day, I saw a number of sea gulls. They glided about effortlessly, but were out of place, out of their natural habitat. Why were they so far from home? There were no fish, crabs, shellfish, or other natural foods on which they subsist. And the gulls were not lost, nor were they wanderers, drifters, shiftless. They were out of place and posed a riddle. In his novel, The Snows of Kilimanjaro, Ernest Hemingway challenges us with a like riddle. We find a frozen tiger high above the tree line. Why did he leave the safety of the jungle? Why did he stray so far from home? I am sure each of us can come up with a reason, and many will be divergent. I transpose to you the idiom that "far from home" can stir within you. What logic surfaces as you ponder? Riddles beset us all. You see, when you wander from life's sweet call of decency, kindness, consideration … like the gulls and the tiger, "far from home", becomes your legacy. When we fail to remain faithful to the innocence of our youth, we all become lost … we stray from that place we ought to be … we drift "far from home". When there is no longer a place that is yours in the world … when you no longer know where your friends are to be found … peace dies, hope shrivels, and heavy hangs the heart. Never get caught so far away from home that you can never find your way back.

On the Threshold of Spring

As you gaze across the countryside, you encounter the frustrating, ambivalent nature of Spring struggling to be born. There is an old saying that goes: "Spring has June in its eyes but January in its heart." And if you look closely outdoors you find this to be true. Chill winds you still encounter ... the sun penetrates but with only a primitive warmth ... green tufts dot the lawn but full verdancy is yet to come ... tree buds are barely noticeable ... the first robin is yet to appear ... and the leaves of Fall, still imbedded in the lower hedges bring on a desolate feeling. It is only the isolated and forlorn forsythia blossoms and garish croci that give rise to what is yet to come. For reasons of its own, March is always reluctant to open the door to April. But have heart. Soon the effulgent land will deracinate winter's gloom and proscribe its unkindness. Do you know that when flowers beckon, they assign little hands that reach inside and uncover and sort out the happy times of your life? Flowers are reminiscent of the innocent laughter of my grandchildren, and their growing, radiant countenance. Long incarcerated bulbs burst forth in a triage of colors and reflected beauty that transforms us into our loving providence. Can you comprehend the fullness of that message? For you see, we disdainfully flick aside winter's turpitude, and with eager eyes and a turgid spirit, we embrace the coming of Spring. Do not let the wait scar your resolve.

An Early Summer Day at the Shore

The sea beckons and we find it difficult to resist her summons. So we travel to our favorite place. Standing on the shore, the surf plays its music of eternity. We dare not speak lest we spoil the magic in her message. Light banks of fog hover in the distance ... on the water the hazy sun is diffuse and crinkled ... the chill wind makes you withdraw your warm thoughts ... and the quick changing weather of early summer never allows you to fully enjoy the scope of the ocean's magnificence. But the sea still casts her legerdemain. I see the deep blue in the eyes of my grandchildren ... their skittering feet in the movement of the sandpipers ... their playful energy in the windy glide of the gulls. The quasi warmth of the sun wraps you in its arms and tugs at thoughts of your childhood ... of barefoot days ... splashing merriment ... unbridled laughter ... and crumbling sandcastles. There are other memories too ... as I look beyond the horizon and see ships ply in the distance ... I am transformed to that young sailor on a man-of-war embroiled in history ... and recall the sea in tempest in all its fury ... the wind moans of death and destruction ... nothing releases power like the sea gone mad ... especially when it exceeds the limits at its command. I am brought back to the present by the gleeful cries of children at play ... the sea becomes sublime and the waves gently kissed by the sun ... you throb with the supreme emotion that only love can bring. And I become quizzical. How old is the sea, do you know? As old as time, I presume, and as new as tomorrow. Do you know we all must come to terms with ourselves sometime? What better place than a warm, sunny, breezy, early summer day? But you see narrow souls cannot admire this beauty because they cannot speak to the imagination. They lack the reflection which is visible in a myriad of utterances of a creative mind.

Where The Seagulls Call Your Name

It was the first warm, sunny day after the "storm of the century" and we visited our favorite seaside vacation place to walk along the shore. The sun was pleasant on your face but Winter's dying presence chilled your hands ... a reminder that Winter was not ready to pass on her reign to Spring. The surf was calm and barely audible. Overhead a lone seagull hovered nearby and called my name ... and the name of all who visit here regularly. In retrospect, I heard that girl in the third grade calling my name in laughter. On a cloud I see her sparkling eyes ... her unforgettable smile ... the freckles ... curly hair ... playful demeanor. At recess we ran, chased and caught each other. It was the way of all children ... our way of showing affection. As we continued our stroll along the beach, the damage of past storms was devastating. Every cottage, dock, seawall, dune - all showed signs of that furious tidal surge. But we looked beyond the damage ... we looked ahead to summer when we would come back to stay longer. The damage would be repaired ... the place would be renewed ... and we would once again feel at home. Home where the surf murmurs incessantly ... the blue sky revels in its brilliance ... the warm sun washes away your worries, anxieties, trivial burdens ... and the gulls call your name all day, every day. But on the drive back home, the huge piles of melting snow reminded you that it was not yet time to don your shorts. But that elusive promise has been made ... the first warm day announced it ... and it will be soon ... sooner than you realize ... and all will be well with the world again. Being by the side of the sea brings on quiet reflection and thoughtful contemplation ... and the seagulls and the surf are the only things I will allow to disturb that silence.

A Rainy Stay in Bermuda

People come to Bermuda, or a like warm-sighted, ocean-beach facility, to be re-energized ... for rest, relaxation ... to seek surcease from life's daily anxieties ... for warm sun to tingle the deep, inner recesses of inspiration ... to gaze upon the soft, demure, blue-green sea that dredges up long forgotten thoughts of endearment ... memories that make you sigh ... make you melancholy ... and squeeze your heart with poignant flutters. To awake to a dull, gray, sunless morning, dampened by wind driven rain, beclouds the merriment of your expectations. The tossing sea loses its luster, and you find it difficult to say kind words. Confinement to your room makes it arduous to uplift your spirit ... to shake free the shackles of daily drudgery you came to forget. You get caught up in a conspiracy of makeshift activity, so the rueful day can pass without too much grumbling ... to keep from grousing about the injudicious selections of the weather gods. The whistle of the acrobatic long-tails is curtailed ... the dampened flowers sag ... the yellow birds are burrowed in ... and the relentless dripping eaves add to the gloom. You rail at the parsimony of Mother Nature in dealing out her sunshine. Yet we are all granted the privacy of our thoughts where no one can venture. Sequestered there is the promise that always, tomorrow will be better. It would be difficult to carry on, had we not possessed that eternal hope ... that responsive cord of fulfilled wishes. The sun at its splendor lies above the rakish cloud cover, and will spill her golden charm when the accounting runs its ledger. You see we are born in the baptism of positive proclamations ... we are made for the long pursuit of redemptive reclamation. Sometimes it doesn't get much better than that. Never, ever, ever, engage your friends in false pleasantries, interspersed with a habitual harangue ... for it only trivializes your worthiness.

September at the Beach

We again answer the irresistible call of the sea ... she beckons and we come. You see, this time of the year, the sea holds many delights ... quiet privacy ... no haze ... skies so clear you can see infinity ... the sun bright and squiggly ... a shimmering apex of coalesced quicksilver struggling to be free ... the raucous roar of the surf that never dies. You dislodge yourself from workday banter. A walk on a lonely stretch of beach unclutters your mind ... graceful gulls keep you company ... they command respect of the wind with their maneuvers ... the chattering surf answers your inquiries. In the distance, young lovers walk hand-in-hand at waters edge ... they find enchantment ... a bonding with the surf whose voice will call them back again and again. At night, the pale mellow moon keeps time to a dancing sea ... a million butterflies with marmalade wings fluttering and shimmering ... a canopy of dreamy stars become the glistening eyes of my grandchildren. Have you tried to comprehend the ceaseless surf as it rumbles on and on? Is it a natural phenomenon, or the mysterious rending voices of past human experiences needing to be heard? Can it be the secret sobs of the world's sorrows ... the mournful moaning of wayward souls ... the gleeful gurgles and goos of smiling babies ... the sweet ancient whispers of lovers ... the aggregate agony of histories battlefield dead ... the song of morning glories ... the tumultuous tremors of tortured innocence ... or is it the drumbeat of conscience to the long silence we lend to the cruelty and injustice we witness? At days end we all sleep soundly here. The surf becomes the collective purring of drowsy kittens. In dreams we capture the endowment, the fulfillment – the promises of lovers everywhere.

Fall – The Winsome Season

Anyone who does not warmly rejoice in the multi-colored genesis of autumn surely has had root canal performed on their aesthetic awakening. The colors of Fall speak all languages ... they offer boundless beauty that charms the soul ... delight in the splendor at sundown ... garner this simple goodness and store it in your reverie. Stroll the warm day amid the splashes of red, orange, yellow, gold, russet ... become the eagle that soars through endless space ... be the hawk that hovers in a singing October sky ... gather the scattered rays of sunshine and sprinkle them wherever you go. This winsome season holds a universal message for all of us ... let the Spirit blow freely ... ride the enterprise of goodness. Be not part of that vulgar fate that withholds kindness ... when we succumb to wrong doing and injustice, we compromise the divine power within us ... and add to the prevailing problem of existing evil and brokenness we see in this life. Tis better to seek serenity in the sacrament of nature ... amid the bold strokes of her leafy mural. Except when disturbed, nature's voice is soft and low. To defile this tranquil beauty with boisterous clamor is the ultimate profanation. Wander slowly amid this luster ... gaze silently at this wonder ... mellifluous expressions will surface ... your jeweled eyes and beaming smile will give your feelings away. I revel in the glimmering shadows of things reflected from the past. I easily surrender to fantasy. That is why, for me, the quiet rustle of murmuring leaves calls out the name of that girl in the third grade ... in the painted panorama, the face of a dream appears ... and I extract the poetry from her eyes ... drink the nectar from her lips ... steal the music from her heart ... then give her back to the angels of love. Although we are apart, we are companions still, because, you see, we never really said goodbye.

Character

The dictionary defines character as: essential quality, moral strength, good reputation. It is the foundation of your mettle. It is the vow we make to ourselves in the innocence of our childhood. Remember when family and friends would ask, "What would you like to be when you grow up"? And we responded: teacher, lawyer, doctor, priest, etc ... all noble aspirations. We hoped to become a beacon ... a source of strength and inspiration ... to help those less fortunate ... to leave an enduring mark on the page of history. Aspirations such as these destined you to become part of that messianic formula that would help the downtrodden rise to another level ... to redeem a suffering humanity. Listen to some prophecies: "A man's character is his guardian divinity." (Heraclitus) "Listen to a man's word and look into the pupil of his eye. How can a man conceal his character?" (Mencius) "Character cannot be developed in ease and quiet. Only through experience of trial and suffering can the soul be strengthened, vision cleared, ambition inspired, and success achieved." (Helen Keller) In the beginning, before he fell, ancient Adam was distinguished by the sweet savior of his character. But how far do you go in bartering with the devil, no matter his disguise? You see bad character is like bad wine ... it is bitter and it reeks ... and it will make you retch. Andrew Greeley writes of an Eastern fable that tells of a magic mirror. It remained clear when the good looked upon it, but became sullied when the impure gazed at it. And what reflection do you experience? All people of good character are enlightened with the Truth. And those without it will always be restless at heart ... and left to twist in the wind to regret the wasted chances. Once again the peace and happiness they seek will remain out of reach. Never, ever, ever, become part of that spurious dichotomy that magnifies the divergence of what you say from what you do.

Reflections on a Christmas Past

We never forget a Christmas. No matter how many have come to pass, we always can recall that special day in our lives. We look back to the simplicity of other days, other times, and chafe at the modern complexity. I try to avoid comparisons, but do you know what I find? It is the gaudiness that saddens me ... the blinking lights that detract from the authenticity of a holiday rife with spiritual meaning. The bells, the holly, mistletoe, the garlands and ornaments add a human dimension that heightens the Christmas spirit. Front yards over-decorated and ablaze with intermittent flashings ... I wonder what they convey? They may bring delight and wonder to the eyes of children ... but verge on nefarious vexations for the faithful. The star that guided the shepherds to the crib still shines for you and me ... to direct us to the peace and hope and promise of that little child. History still struggles to define meaning of that particular moment ... and does it still hold true today. Christmas is a Feast of Kindness. Do not be part of the pervasive evil that surrounds us ... do not demean those around you with uncaring and hurtful behavior ... do not disparage those in your charge. It is these actions that steal the peace from our lives, our homes and our community. Christmas restores the harmony in our lives that was meant to be. It beckons us to the mountainside ... to touch a star ... to give rise to the melody of the sun ... to edify the soul in music ... to catch some feathered snowflakes of happiness. It is our human imperfections that interfere with our noble aspiration! For only vulgar people have base motives. You see we all come home at Christmas and become the children we remember. Shalom.

Take Time for Spring

Though winter lingers still, the first green shoots appear in the ground and whisper of spring. For too many nights we have heard the winter wind brush against the window. But what a delightful sound when spring calls your name. A lone crocus nudges from the snow ... snowbells sway in the breeze. Close your eyes and you feel the soft breath of spring ... you see daffodils nod and tulips smile ... and fill you with a secret mirth. Soon it will be time to seek that quiet pause ... to sit in your yard and lift your head to the sky. Let the warm sun cradle your face ... your thoughts become easy ... your cares released. And you become a child again. Spring, when a touch of love is in the air. In the frothy clouds I see the sweet face of that girl in the third grade ... I hear the music in her heart ... her laughter makes the flowers grow ... in her eyes the sunlight of innocence ... in her hands the flush of first love. I feel her touch still ... and I remember that day when she said, "yes" to our first kiss. Like a haunting love song, that kiss dances in my dreams. How I miss the yesterdays I left behind ... all the springs when I wondered where butterflies go when it rains ... that wonderland of buds and flowers and birds and the soft green grass of home. May I give you some advice? This spring talk some but listen more. No one is born wise ... it is the gathering of experience with time that brings on wisdom. We all wait for that perfect moment in our lives ... but because of fear and caution ... the desire for all risks to disappear ... we do not trust ourselves enough ... and that perfect moment never comes. Because we are all endowed with a special gift, I will make you a promise. If you take time this spring ... enfolded in a quiet peace ... precious memories of innocent love of yesterday will come to you ... a time when your hearts were full of dreams and promise ... and a place deep down within you will sigh ... and love will seek its sweet release.

A Cold Day in May at the Shore

It is the small, still voice of the sea that beckons ... it calls and we answer ... to be by the side of the sea ... to feel the breezy expansiveness ... to bask in that thought-filled aura of yesterday's pleasant memories ... you smile and lighten your heart. It was cold for May ... it is windy and chilly ... the sea is boisterous and will not allow you to speak. The surf is ponderous ... it rattles the stones and carries the sand away ... the spray is scattered like snow in a blizzard. You reach for the promise that lies beyond the horizon and it sets you free ... it releases you from the tight-rope of anxiety ... your mind scurries to join the seagulls in flight ... to drift, unfettered, undisciplined, unattached. And you claim all of this for yourself ... because you paid for it ... paid for it by the many trials, troubles, and tribulations ... those harsh demands of life. You walk the deserted beach and feel haunted ... whispers from that inner-self keep prodding, "Are you the person you promised to be?" We journey here often ... for the serenity ... to calm misbegotten fears ... ill-conceived paradoxes ... presupposed calamities. It is here that small moments of our lives become visionary and dream-filled ... hopeful innocence a basis for future acclaim. The stillness of the twilight hour watches the sun chase the daylight away ... and the shadows call the night to appear. The moon comes out to play its age-old magic on the surface ... like a million, silver coated fireflies, playing hide-and-seek. Time to sleep ... to enjoy the quiet pastime of a solitary dream ... to caress the peace we all so dearly desire ... to come out of the shadows and stand in the warm sunlight of affection. e. e. cummings writes, "For whatever we lost (like a you or a me) it's always ourselves we find in the sea."

A Trip to the Canadian Rockies: Scenery That Takes Your Breath Away

After viewing vacation literature, we decided on a trip to the Canadian Rockies. Pictures of snow-capped mountains and emerald lakes made this decision easy. The trip began in Toronto. We were treated to a tour of this burgeoning city, the financial capitol of Canada. Highlights included the tallest building in the world, the Toronto Tower, and the military officer's club that featured cannons used in the Battle of Waterloo, and the cockpit of the plane of the Red Baron, Baron Von Ricktofen, Germany's air ace of World War I, shot down by a young Canadian, Tom Brown.

Boarding the train for a three day excursion across Canada was the beginning of a fabulous ten days of sightseeing into the grandeur of our neighbor to the north. Three days of rolling countryside that included miles of forests, lakes, rivers, prairies, and mountain ranges, exposed a country still undiscovered and still open to pioneering and development. Train accommodations were deluxe, including private roomettes, first class dining car, observation deck, and cocktail lounge.

Arriving in Jasper, our western destination, was a prelude to the mountain extravagance we were to experience. It was good to leave the train in Jasper, and be transported to the lodge at Jasper National Park. Surrounded by mountains and overlooking an emerald green lake, all rooms at the lodge offer a view that defies description. One just looks in awe, and is inspired by the beauty. The gem at Jasper Park Lodge is the glacier capped Edith Cavell Mountain, named after a Canadian heroine of World War I. Also unforgettable, was dining at the lodge with a choice of four exquisite restaurants.

Two days at the lodge over, we boarded a bus which took us to Peyto Lake, Lake Louise, and finally to Banff Springs Hotel. The bus ride was a panorama of emerald green rivers, lakes, snow-capped mountains, and a bevy of wild life (deer, mountain goats and wild sheep). The highlight of this trip was a visit to the Athabasca Glacier in the Columbia Ice Field. Boarding an all-terrain vehicle, we were transported to the ridge of the glacier, where we were allowed to explore the moving ice-cap that stretched two miles across, extended four miles in length, and was 1000 feet thick. Walking on this glacier in windy 50° temperature is an experience that you will never forget.

At Banff, the hotel is ringed by spectacular mountains, and brushes the Bow River, which runs close by. In the quiet of the night, you can hear the rush of the Bow River Falls that are enormous in their natural power and beauty. The highlight at Banff is a ride in a gondola up to the top of Sulphur Mountain, which rises 7500 feet and overlooks Banff National Park. The view is absolutely breathtaking, and spiritually inspiring. Accommodations and dining were fabulous at the hotel.

Our final day was a motor coach ride to Calgary, where we passed some of the grounds of the "88 Winter Olympics. We said good-bye to some of our traveling companions at Calgary Airport, and caught a plane to Montreal, then onto LaGuardia. From there we limousined home with our hearts full of memories of the gorgeous and remarkable scenery of the Canadian Rockies. It is a place that we plan to go back to, and soon.

A Reunion

The fundamental priority of friends to gather, never changes. So our old neighborhood had a reunion last month. Friends, neighbors, from the 1930's, 40's, and 50's, gathered to renew old friendships, to recall special moments. Some of us had not seen each other in fifty years. And they came from Alabama, Florida and California. Do you know what reunions are about? They are about joining that part of our lives that we have become ... to that part we left behind ... to reconcile that lost dimension. We all belonged to that special fraternity that has endured two of the greatest calamities of modern history: The Depression, which made harsh demands on our lives ... and World War II, which made the harshest demand of them all. We were caught up in a web of history ... and these events happened on our watch as a generation. Surviving those tough times forged our character ... and formed the matrix of our existence. The reunion was a time to ride the dream back to when we were young ... to recall special moments that tug at your heart. While lost time is intractable, memories are not. We all came home that night ... home to our past ... home to your youth ... home to magic memories. All generations have a unique identity. But our generation was marked with a special sign. We had two choices: you could lie awake at night and weep for your lost opportunities; or you could overcome adversity ... and rise to a level of achievement that far exceeded your expectations. And that is the choice we all made. It was a long time ago, but it felt like yesterday ... you reached out to touch the moments, and they touched you back ... moments that get into your heart and never get out. We were fragile, gray, stooped, wizened ... but inside we were all young again. We regained our bounce, our sparkle, our vigor. And for one shining evening, we wandered down the path of yesterday, and reveled in the pleasures of what has been.

At the Sea in September

It is still warm by the sea in late September … summer gives you its final sweet caress … and a soft autumn wind calls. The sun weaves a glittering mosaic … thoughts are warm and memories gentle … the surf repeats itself over and over … the blue sky offers a friendly embrace … and you try to fathom the awesome dimension that spreads beyond what the eye can see. You walk along the deserted shore and gaze at the calmness. That guarded secret place opens the door and you liberate the best in yourself … you become Spirit and light and fire and wind and truth. You are free … free to go … free to become what you promised … free to dance with destiny … free to become truly yourself. The sea calls from beyond the horizon in faint whispers and echoes … and mitigates your terrors, rigidities, hesitations. You rid yourself of narrow fears and timid anxieties … old misconceptions fade … the pains, failures, rejections, are mollified. The sea in September touches the finest, sharpest point in your personality … the very core of your identity … and tells us we can be far more than we are … you become aware of possibilities in yourself which were never apparent before. What lies beyond the limits? Is this your occasional encounter with immortality? The sea tells us that intimate vulnerability is the first principle of loving … it is required to awaken the spark of divinity that is in each of us. You reveal yourself … and in that revelation you discover the possibility of something greater. The September sea never loses the uniqueness of its message … when you hear it call, do not fail to respond … for if you do, it will cost you those golden moments where you become more loving to those closest to you … and you will remain trapped in your weaknesses when they come to steal your truth.

By the Sea, By the Sea,
By the Beautiful Sea

For late June, the day had the feel of October. It was a lazy sun that was slow to warm. The breeze was cool, the sea strangely calm. The surf was soft and spoke in a low voice, as if bewildered. Clouds carried a dark side that I did not wish to interpret. I was mystified by the absence of birds. Where do the seagulls go on a day like this? People walking the beaches wore sweatshirts and wind breakers. Some defied the circumstances and dared to sun, trying for a welcome tan. There were few whitecaps … the air clear … and offered unlimited vision. Far on the horizon, ships slowly passed. As you gazed beyond the reach of reality, where sky meets the sea, warm thoughts of yesterday danced in your reverie. How could anyone harbor mean thoughts in this setting? Trivial animosities are not borne here. Petty jealousies take flight. The dancing sun on the gently rolling sea, blends the colors of our grandchildren's eyes, and you could hear their gleeful cries at play. You reach out to hug them, and their music and poetry wells in your heart. You cross the bridge that spans the memories, and you sigh with happiness. This extraordinary blend of nature's culminations is sometimes too much for the mind to encompass. Alone, and at a distance … free from outside distractions … you choose to face yourself and ask the hard questions we all find difficult to answer without compromise: Am I everything I promised to be? Do I stand strong with clean hands and straight eyes? Do I sleep with the peace of innocent childhood? Have I enriched the legacy of generosity and kindness? Is my faith a queasy thing that quavers in the face of adversity? Have I been faithful to the fundamental call to "love one another"? Or are we all three steps from wistful, and apprehensive about what lies beyond the rise of tomorrow? By moonlight, I take one more look before retiring, and on my face I feel the vicarious etchings of angel wings.

Time

Do you know that time is an awesome responsibility for all of us? And comes the judgment, you and I are going to have to account for every minute? I broach the subject because I am reminded of a poem from my student days:

> Time by minutes slips away
> First the hour then the day
> Small the daily loss appears
> Yet it soon amounts to years

Isn't it a shame how adept we can become at killing time? For clock-watchers, time hangs heavy. For others, night comes too quickly. Which of these applies to you? For children, the days are long with gathering experience. As we grow old, the value of time becomes vivid. You see, lost time is intractable. And time does not deal gently with everyone. This very moment, this very hour, this day, is the most important time in your life. Use it in wisdom. But we don't. We foolishly seem to be saving our deepest emotions ... we keep our vocabulary of tenderness in reserve ... for that "one big shining moment" in our lives ... that great prize of fame and fortune to come over the horizon ... that worldly ecstasy of handfuls of golden coins caressing our fingers. But it somehow manages to elude us for endless tomorrows. Can't you see the greater rewards in small deeds that avail themselves to us right now? Like making a child laugh ... bringing a smile to the lonely ... a comforting touch to the ill ... a consoling hug to the mournful ... a moment of peace to the troubled. These are the treasures of substance. And they attach no waiting period. You must use the gifts that time brings. In my mind, our greatest temptation is wanting to escape the limits of time ... to remain young ... to live forever ... to be sure of a place in heaven. But that has not been apportioned to us. For only God alone stands beyond the boundaries of time. And it is by our worthy use of time that we reconcile with Him.

At the Shore in Autumn

To be by the side of the sea in late Autumn is a unique experience. The throngs of summer vacationers are gone … and only the hardy venture forth. Fishermen outnumber the tourists … and the fading warmth of the sun tries to subdue the tart nip in the air. There is a different dimension to the sparkle of the sun on the ocean's surface … it glows with a lesser intensity … muted and stunted as it diffuses in broad expanses. No one walks barefoot on the cool sand … but seagulls gather in groups and sit in sunny areas, relishing the faint warmth of the Fall sun. Few boats ply off shore … having retreated with the summer. There is a look and feel in the air that signals a change in seasons. Cottages and summer homes are shuttered … children's happy voices are hushed … the wind and surf soft … the cloudless sky as blue and fresh as a new found promise. You are caught up in a flush of memories that carry you back … back to a time when you were young and innocent. Something tugs at your heart … and you see that face of the girl in the third grade … her eyes … her smile … her touch … her laugh … the magic of that first kiss. You don't remember saying goodbye … but you went in different directions … and you wonder where she is now. You chastise yourself for letting her get away. The nights are different … darkness comes early … the stars and moon are brighter and sharper … full of hope and wishes. Sleep comes easy as you listen to the lullaby of the surf. And you dream of Elysian fields where happiness is born … and it never, ever, ever, can be taken away from you.

The Leaves of Autumn Leave Us

The leaves of autumn leave me loquacious. My kinship with nature is deeply manifested, therefore must be conveyed. Summer has left us, and we are enriched by a new season. No longer green, the landscape is embellished by a blending of colors. Colors so rich and appealing, they ring bells of joy in your soul. I become a youthful larrikin and frolic in the countryside. Only the doleful cannot find merriment here. Ride the wind and let your eyes feast on the beauty that surrounds you. Paintings sometimes do not truly honor what your eyes perceive and the spirit interpret. Surely you are not one of those who are not placated by the fruits of Fall? Woe to those who do not find solace and cannot salve a wounded vanity. Hard frost has made the flowers bid their last farewell. However, there is not sadness. They only sleep until they rise again. Drifting back to when my time was young, it was an autumn of: shocks of corn, the aroma of burning leaves, Indian summer, apple cider, unharvested pumpkins, and football. But the most endearing memories are of the breathtaking hillside along the Connecticut River. You see, the multi-colored genesis of autumn releases your blitheful spirit, and encumbers the wild will never. Feelings of warmth, joy, and hope direct the positive thrust of your life away from the melancholy. Although we are on the bold threshold of winter, do not despair. There is goodness no matter the season. And I revel in the poetry of that promise. Do you know that you and I are bound by the tendrils of love and affection? Never, ever, ever, empty your heart of generosity, kindness, and compassion. Not even for a moment. A barren soul is an unforgivable offense against humanity and God. Be ready always to regenerate your capacity to love, to share, to laugh, to smile, to cry, to care. To always promulgate the noble bondage of love is central to our mission. And when you love, you must do so absolutely and unconditionally. Have your autumns of the past been as abundant as mine? Do you wax nostalgic in the bright blue of October?

Have You Seen a Child's
Eyes at Christmas?

The tree was trimmed and lighted. Presents placed beneath reflected the myriad of colors from the trimmings. It was late and the house warm, silent and somnolent. Overcome with a tranquil weariness, it was time to sit, close your eyes, and immerse yourself in the hush and stillness on the eve of Christmas. The soothing refrain of carols, muted by the crisp night air, wafted dreamily through the room. Thoughts of Christmas Past, when you were a child, appear in your mind and fill your soul with a peace that only the Christ Child can bring. And you recall a poem you read long ago:

> "Lord, in the quiet of this hour
> Let me feel your love and power."

You need to feel the power of this Holy Night because power is born of silence and presence.

Christmas is for children. And you recall the eagerness of your own childhood. And how you scrambled to your stocking to see what Santa brought. Only now your thoughts are of your own children, now grown, and the grandchildren who will be coming tomorrow. Before retiring, you turn down the lights, and through the window, check the twinkling stars in the clear, frigid night. You wonder if that bright star in the eastern sky is the same one that shown over the manger so long ago. Then you dream of Christmas symbols: silver bells, tender lullabies, three kings, angels singing, evergreen, icy window panes, and snowflakes that dance in the wind. Asleep, you find the inner peace that is the promise of Christmas.

Morning comes quickly, and the knock on the door tells you that the family is gathering. You greet your children warmly, then reach for those squiggly, squirmy, squealing bundles of energy. You hold them close and hug and squeeze and kiss. In return their soft eyes convey the answer sought by civilizations throughout history – the meaning and purpose of life.

Dinner over, presents are distributed. You ignore your own to watch the young ones. They scamper and shriek, and jump and reach, and point and wiggle; paper flies and cries of glee fill the room. And then you notice their eyes – wide, glistening, dazzling, and sparkling. Eyes that reflect the innocent, inviolate, and pure promise of that child born so long ago in a place so far away. Then you catch a glimpse of your grown children, now parents themselves, and they see it too. And as your eyes meet, there is mutual acknowledgement, warm and loving, that deep in all of us lives a bit of a child. And in our dreams, our hearts go home at Christmas – that home of our childhood we remember and love so much.

God bless the children one and all for to them belongs the kingdom.

Is There Anything Nice to be Said About Winter?????

It wasn't so long ago that we cursed the dreadful heat and humidity of summer. And now as the wind chill reaches minus 15 degrees and rakes our faces and ices our toes, we curse the morbid winter. Gray, windy, stormy days make us all less friendly, more withdrawn. Sweaters, heavy coats, earmuffs, gloves, boots, seem such a bother. Early darkness, short daylight, going to work and coming home in the dark, seems such a pain. When the sun does shine, enjoy it quickly, because it fades too soon and is smothered in an Arctic sky. Does winter compel cruelty?

You wistfully recall your days as a youth when you frolicked in the snow, skated on the frozen pond, and sledded down the icy hill. Oh! The exuberance of youth, and it's never ending theme of fun and folly. I find myself going back to my youth, no matter the season. Father Andrew Greeley writes in one of his books, "You don't understand that the rest of your life will be a search to rediscover the origins of your childish high spirits." Father Greeley calls this the "tenderness of the cosmos". All of us in our adult lives conduct this search for the secret of happiness, and for the tender and affectionate source of that happiness. That is why the winters of our childhood seem like such a pleasant, happy, fun-filled time.

Is it age that changes all of that? Is growing old so painful that it diminishes our ability to find something good of winter? I think one of life's greatest pleasures is to see a snow covered landscape, untouched by human necessity. Deep, fresh, glistening, bright snow, marked only by animal tracks, that keeps its glossy luster for long periods of time. And at night, when the moon bathes the snow in tenderness, you feel the essence of spirituality. It is mindful of the necessary reconciliation of the soul before grace can be granted.

It is we adults who constantly complain of storms, and chills, and snow tires, and heating costs, and snowplows, and aching backs from shoveling. We flee south to the sun and do not dare plan a trip by car until spring. But if you search your memory, you will find one of life's greatest treasures is a "walk in the snow with someone you love".

Let me use some adjectives to describe what most people feel about this terrible time of the year: Winter is cold-hearted, sullen and sad. It is filled with melancholy days, wailing winds, naked woods, brown meadows, and frozen ponds. Winter is the lonely season – short days when sun is rarely seen. February is a little girl with her first valentine. March is a tomboy with tousled hair … April, wet and pretentious.

This article is not for ski buffs or cold weather lovers. For them winter is never long enough. For the rest of us, the next time that you shiver and bundle up against the cold, think of warm and sunny days that lie ahead. Spring – when all things are made young and we are deemed heady with thoughts of love, and life, and laughter.

If I Had a Great Notion ...

If I had a great notion do you know what I would do? I would be tempted to make everyone's dream come true. But let us analyze the reality of that wish, and ponder the implications. We would all become rich. We would all live in a castle on the mountaintop. We would be above counsel. Nobody would work. Nannies would raise the children. Caring for the grandchildren would be a bother. For breakfast it would be lobster, strawberries, and champagne: for lunch, caviar. And for dinner, medallions of mink nurtured on lotus leaves. When the president would come to dinner, we would seat him at the far end of the table because he would not be as important. We would become part of that surging crowd who constantly seek the painted promise of fun – acarpous conditions to sow seeds of motivation to morality, maturity, and missionary zeal. No longer would we embrace the lame, the halt, and the blind: conditions that evoke acts of kindness that keep us human. Their presence would interrupt our comfort and disturb our conscience. Our faith would be lessened because our belief would become that heaven could be bought. We would become the sum of our possessions - a most empty achievement when you can show no human gain. When you become preoccupied with self, all concerns turn inward. The golden thread of wisdom portends that the challenge of adversity develops character. And life devoid of character diminishes the soul. The secret to happiness is being able to distinguish between what you need and what you want; what you have and what you desire. Although you may think so, they are not the same. It is my opinion that the only prize worth seeking is to slip the surly bonds of yourself and touch the face of others. Therefore, if I had a great notion, what do you think I would do? Better still, what would you do??

Resolutions for 1995

The past year should not be a problem for you, unless you plan to repeat it. Can you live with your misbegotten deeds of 1994? Let us converse about the coming year, and the resolutions you plan to abide by. By nature, we do not comply with our New Year's resolutions … we make them in earnest, but blithely discard them when they become an inconvenience. Benjamin Franklin said, "Resolve to perform what you ought … perform without fail what you resolve." Shabby gentility is the lot of the imprudent. There is nothing more tragic than an empty life … those who live on pretense … small minded and transparent … those who go through life wearing a mask and quarrel with themselves … product of a troubled mind … and troubled soul. Want to change? Then start on the seventh day of Christmas … January 1st, 1995 … that day that you give to your true love, "seven swans a swimming". Resolve to articulate the spirit of kindness and compassion … of understanding and tolerance. Nothing defines better the nature of your character … and character defines who and what you really are. You see, love is out there, and it wants us. Do you know that rudeness and spite leave addictive traces in our lives? Do not confine your warmth and tenderness to the holiday season … spread it throughout the year. Make it a period of hope and promise … from within yourself … to beyond yourself. It is time to sing a new song … that sweet warble that ensures our own dignity … and the dignity of others. The invective of unkindness diminishes us all … like a thief, it steals from us the peace we so dearly seek. You see, nothing in life is worth a moment, if we lose sight of eternity. On what side of the chasm will we find you, same time, next year?

Spring

Ah!! Be still my dancing heart!! This is the feeling that besets us all by the wondrous smell of springtime when fields are in bloom. Right from the first sign, when the crocuses and snowbells peek from the snow, until the daffodils and tulips nod approval in a gentle breeze. Then the first robin and blue jay appear, followed by a pair of wild doves. And when the returning mockingbird attacks the cat, the feeling really sets in. The greening of the lawn proliferates and spreads rapidly. Pussy willows are bursting and the maize-like florid forsythia tries to grab center stage. The rising hyacinth trumpets their expectations. The earth is dark and moist and promises a bounty. You suddenly realize that winter is fading like congealed snow that melts in your hand. You see winter ravages the land with impunity. But spring brings flowers of new life that are examples of eternal seduction and poetry of reproduction. The sun bathes you in analgesic warmth, and you release a murmur of relief as you shed the robe of winter. At a time like this, how can you express anger at the unpleasant arrangement of little things in your daily life? If you do, then you become part of that genre of effusive malcontents. Enclosed in this verdancy, you dream of days past, when as a child you enjoyed the aesthetic inclinations of the season, but the depth of appreciations eluded you. Do you know that dreams build their nest in the drowsy dark cave of the mind, awaiting special occasions such as this to be recalled? At times we all live in make-believe, that sunny country of imagination. You see love is born in the sanctuary of ourselves, and flowers that blossom in the heart never fade. Take time to enjoy the beauty of spring. It will make you stir to your own impulse, and fill your heart with lyrics of romance.

Teachable Moments Amid the Flowers of Late Summer

Iris, lilacs, rhododendrons, mountain laurel, and azaleas have blossomed and faded. Asters, tiger lilies, mums and dahlias are now showing their colors. They are competing with each other and spare no effort in trying to evoke expressions of joy and appreciation. Roses are proliferating and defy modesty to proclaim their reign. Because of the overabundance of rain, this year's flowers lack luster, confidence, sheen, and all too soon wither. They succumb too easily to nature's harsh hand. I want to berate them for lacking spunk, but Mother Nature is too formidable a foe for me. The grandchildren (Michael, Brian, and Joey, who will soon be joined by Billy and Nicholas) come and in their perpetual motion and never ending supply of energy, invade the garden and pluck the flowers. In their desire to please Grandpa ("Pop-Pop") and Grandma ("Mop-Mop"), they lay their offerings in our lap - smiling, clapping, jumping, proud of their achievement and happy to be giving. And this becomes a "teachable moment". You hold them close, hug and kiss them to reaffirm your love. Then softly, quietly, you try to impress upon them that there is a purpose, a time, and a method for flowers to be gathered. And you will teach them. Do you know that innocence can never violate innocence? For harm or evil to be concluded, egregious intent must be the perpetrator. But children are above intent. For they have not yet acquired the irascible nature of adulthood - that twilight of emotion that finds us in constant conflict of right or wrong, good and evil. Life for us grown-ups is a steady application of morality in our daily regime, as adjudicated by the good results of "teachable moments" that we pass on to children everywhere. Whether it applies to picking flowers, throwing objects, pushing others, sharing things, or listening to counsel. Although we are generations older and wiser, we cannot erase our own experiences in history. But we can learn from them and use them as the basis for teaching. You see the splendor of wisdom never sleeps. Can you recall some "teachable moments" in your life?

Autumn's Gifts

Nature's rich tapestry ... that package of colors we call autumn ... fills us with warmth and memories. It puts a sheen in your eyes and a smile in your heart. Autumn is that tandem gentry of heart and soul. The blazing hillside sings ... it sings the melancholy songs of love ... it sings of faded pleasant memories of our childhood ... of first love ... of first kiss ... of newfound infatuations ... and treasured innocence we constantly seek to reclaim. In the panoramic blend of colors ... of varied hues of red, orange, gold, yellow, brown ... we see the faces we can never forget ... the luster in eyes that sear our memories. In the priceless silence you hear the voices ... voices that rise above the limits of human longing ... voices that were constant reminders to guard against what you shouldn't become. The beauty of autumn speaks words that reach the depth of our lives. It reaches personal boundaries no one should exceed. It makes that particular dimension of our personality call out from the shadows. It is the leaves of gold and skies of purest blue that bring out the bright light of our best nature ... it beckons the love ... the warm friendship ... the infectious kindness ... the redeeming merits that bring about peace in our day ... and fragments of happiness to those around us. Strange thing, happiness ... you see we all seek it with grim determination, but few really attain it. Do you know why? Because they seek it where it cannot be found.

The Scarlet Banner of Autumn

The colors of autumn speak all languages ... they write love letters to us all. There is seduction in the foliage that breeds memory and desire ... in the brilliance of the hillside, all things are possible ... and for a moment you regain your innocence. All things point home in October ... it is the sweet/sad yearning for Indian summer ... where Spring and Fall blend into a warm melancholy ... where the splendor of romance never sleeps. The beauty of autumn is the shimmer of liquid milieu ... of brown and red and orange and yellow and scarlet, that your heart applauds ... your spirit sings the sentimental songs of love ... it offers the promise of happiness ... the hope, the dream, the search, the wonder. You must treasure this great masterpiece for it dispels the haunting fear that happiness will elude you ... or someone will set the bounds of beauty. You must admire and appreciate this bounty ... take fire in your bosom ... reap the sweet harvest of passionate friendship ... and ask, "What is your secret?" The ventriloquy of falling leaves will soon trumpet the onset of winter ... that time where our soft, pliable nature turns to stone ... that sullen and sad season of sweeping gloom that steals from us our patience and resolve. You see, those who use that constant, tired utterance, "I'm too busy", to avoid the perfection of nature's artistry, verge on sinfulness ... their reliance on that falsehood robs them of life's riches and rewards. James Thurber says, "The hellbent will get where they are going." And Seneca writes, "People think to be busy is proof of happiness." There is infinite worth in every moment because they represent eternity ... and the passing moments of colorful Fall are the only thing you can be sure of.

Thanksgiving

During the month of November, we experience the gentle warmth of Indian summer, and the ruthless, biting winds of Winter's prelude. However, November is best recorded as a celebration of Thanksgiving - a holiday whereby a turkey dinner and all the trimmings are enjoyed at family gatherings everywhere. It has its origin in an Indian and Puritan banquet that was held as an expression of gratitude for the bounty of the land during the harsh early times they endured together. And that translation exists today. It is a noble and endearing cause we remember, but the holiday really has a deeper and more profound assignation. It is a time for genuine reciprocity, of sharing, caring, loving relationships of family, friends, neighbors, and associates … all of those who have touched our lives in so many ways. It is a time to extend one's hand, heart, and hugs to each other in a true and abiding demonstration of sincerity and solicitude. It is a time to render dissolute the petty grievances, animosities, jealousies, envy, and vindictiveness that we are all capable of harboring. These flaws in our character are bitter seeds of an iniquitous harvest. In a thimble full of days, Advent presages Christmas, which is even a greater and loving promise of radiant goodness and generosity. Never, ever, ever, let your love for others languish. You see, Lady Wisdom makes her own rounds, seeking those worthy of her. She sits at your gate and is present to those capable of sustaining love. When she knocks on your door, do not deny her.

The Cold Wind of Unkindness

President George Bush, in his inaugural speech in 1989, promised to provide the leadership that would bring about a "kinder and gentler" nation. Like many of his election promises, they were fraudulent. Therefore it passes unto all of us, as individuals, to fulfill that pledge to bring the essence of human compassion into that small sphere where we live and toil. The Greeks, in their ancient wisdom, knew the tremendous human cost of unkindness. Listen to what they said:

- "There is no sickness worse for me, than words that to be kind must lie." (Aeschylus)
- "You can accomplish by kindness, what you cannot by force." (Publilius Syrus)
- "One who knows how to show kindness, will be a friend better than any possession." (Sophocles)

You see it is the eternal pessimists ... the doom-sayers ... those of solemn countenance and morbid mouthings ... those who forgot how to smile ... whose voices drip with acrimony ... they spin false webs of maternalism ... but their true nature undone, you find a jackal of perfidy. The universal message for all of us is to exude that internal coagulation of the need to be good ... decent ... moral ... gentle. Do not suborn your innate kindness in contumely, graceless rhetoric. Be always marked by the sign of sincerity, not sophistry. Your need for self-fulfillment will never be realized ... your quest for peace in our day will never come to fruition ... unless you extend to others the never ending need of kindness and caring. Do as Lincoln asked: "Call forth the better angels of your nature."

The Children of Christmas

At Christmas time we all become children again. An enclave of memories unfolds and reveals the story of childhood untold. Out of the sequestered portals of yesterday, emerges our ebullient, elfish selves – rolling in the snow, throwing snowballs, sliding down a hill, and making a snowman. You are filled with an exhilaration you will never experience again until you see it in the eyes of your children and grandchildren. It is Christmas Eve, it is late, all are asleep, all is still. You are alone with soft lights of the tree. How you treasure this quiet time. Love is everywhere. The most moving moments of our lives sometimes find us without words. The heart stirs to the holiness and beauty of this night. Do you know that night is the mother of counsel? You close your eyes, and in the tenderness of the stars, the muted strains of an angelic choir spirits your reverie to the song, "Silent Night". You do not dare search for the source of the music. You drift to a faraway hillside where shepherds are restless as the brightness of a certain star disturbs the sleep of sheep. You finally begin to fathom the messianic message of the babe in the manger. Your grown children will be coming tomorrow with the grandchildren. At Christmas you will always see your children as toddlers. You recall other years when they hurried down to the tree. And only you alone will ever understand the voice in their eyes, the warmth of their hugs, the love in their kisses, and the happiness in their smiles. You know you will live it again tomorrow in the radiant and innocent faces of the grandchildren. You drift upstairs to bed, and somehow you cannot erase that smile in your heart. Time has divisions to mark its passage. But childhood memories of Christmas defy the clock, the calendar, the centuries. Above all else these memories endure. Now close your eyes and see yourself at the age and time you remember best. Never ever let yourself outgrow Christmas. Never lose the simple vision of that child you once were.

Spring: When Love Stories Are Born

"Blossom by blossom Spring begins", so writes Charles Swinburne. And when daffodils nod … and tulips smile … and warm, sunny days herald a ringing melody of nature's symphony … a touch of love fills the air. Neil Diamond croons, "Some things never change, like saying I love you." In Spring, love lingers, though our days grow old. Memories never age … and you alone will always hear the dear and silent things only lovers' lips can tell. Love is that tender message that words alone cannot convey. It is woven into the flowers of Spring … it is frailer than the spider's web … yet stronger than the bonds of steel. In Spring, all our fancies turn to love … pleasant thoughts … sweet words … warm sentiments. A soft, touching, lifting tune reaches inside and nudges your heart. Put all your small vexations away … stifle your sad sighs. Render dissolute your reciprocal desire for malice, envy, and retribution. Old sins cast long shadows … they keep you restless and unfulfilled … and conscience is a stern, uncompromising witness. Recall the innocent love of yesterday … when hearts were full of dreams … and the glow and warmth of that tender touch, was the shining truth that lit your way. The radiance of affection comes only to those who answer love's knock on your heart in Spring. The next time you are with your dear one, tell her what Shirley Bassey sings, "I never, never, never, never, want to be in love with anyone else but you."

Early Summer Makes the Heart Sing

The crocuses, early snowdrops, and snow glories are gone. Daffodils, tulips, and hyacinth have been picked and are generating for next spring. Dahlias have been planted - they are restless and full of promise. Rose bushes and dogwoods are preparing to burst forth. Daisies, dianthus, and lilacs have awakened, and are readying their symmetrical show of beauty. Don't you feel exhilarated at the sight of new grass, so fresh and green and soft? And when the warm sun, in its life giving fullness, filters into the deepest recesses of your being, doesn't it make your heart want to sing the silent song of love? Father Andrew Greeley, in his book, <u>Confessions of a Parish Priest</u>, asks, "Is summer a delusion or a sacrament?" He poignantly circumscribes to us the sweet / sad vulnerability of summer love we have all experienced. You will find me quoting Fr. Greeley quite often. Anyone who writes with such spiritual perspicacity and candor, warrants quoting. Don't you feel liberated from the icy imprisonment winter imposes? I seem to be full of questions today. But what raises questions more, than to witness the splendor that a changing season brings? Is it the conversion of the bleak and barren countryside into a picturesque landscape that brings on an added grace? Or perhaps it is the treasure of seeing a butterfly softly kiss the tulips? It is then that you feel the silken memory of someone you love, reach inside and tenderly nudge your heart. We should all rejoice at this glorious time of the year. It brings the flowers that are a monument to the fulfillment of love. Early summer brings forth individual, redeeming resolutions within us that mandate we promise to be more kind, more caring, more considerate, more gracious, in our daily interchange with each other. Let me close by recalling from past readings, author unknown. "Summer renders dissolute the restraints people impose on themselves to refrain from loving. It lessens the severities of the hardened."

The End of Summer at the Shore

Summer retreated yesterday on the heels of a violent thunderstorm, slashing rainfall, and thunderous surf that shook the ground. A bright sun and chill wind greeted us in the morning. A light jacket was needed to walk at waters edge. Bluefish were feeding off shore, and the sea gulls were in a frenzy. The sea had calmed, and the sun glittered on the surface, like fireflies generating high intensity luminescence. You look up and down miles of beach ... you count very few people ... you finally feel this is yours ... your own haven. It is treasured time for quiet reflection and you apply a spiritual stamp of approval. The endless horizon elicits tranquil thoughts of youthful innocence. You see your child-self romping and squealing in the surf and sand ... with no thoughts of growing up and what the muddled world of adulthood has in store. I still feel the softness of that first kiss ... effulgent throb of my heart in first love ... those winsome, sparkling eyes ... the symphonic laughter ... timeless feelings ... forever rapture ... crowned by the endowed innocence of every child. Sitting here, writing this, being older and wiser and somber ... that same child stirs inside ... and tugs, and tugs, and tugs at your heart ... and reminds you, that at least for a little while ... at this place ... in this setting ... it is all right to once again romp and squeal in the sand and surf ... for only you can hear.

The Freshness of the Ocean Breeze

We arrive at our seaside vacation place at noon. We dress hurriedly and head for the beach. The freshness of the ocean breeze holds the heat of the day at bay. The sea is tranquil and the surf moderate. The sun stings your eyes as it reflects off the water. The sand is warm but the water cold, and it shrivels and tingles the skin of your feet. People are everywhere and for the moment, you wish you could sweep them away. For they interfere with your communication with the sea. We walk the far reaches to the steady chorus of the surf. Puffy clouds dreamily drift by. The sun on your shoulders is comforting. You finally feel free, unchained from workday bondage. Multi-colored stones - worn round by constant grating, lie everywhere. We stop to observe the graceful flight of seagulls, and secretly wish we could fly with them. Young lovers walk by holding hands, and you turn back the calendar and see yourself. Far away from the crowd we stop, and the sea, sun, sky, sand, ships, surf, stones, and seagulls come together and nuzzle your soul, like the warm hugs of your grandchildren. If you believe in your heaven, your Nirvana, your Elysian fields, then this place, this scene, this moment, is a prelude. Do you wonder why we keep coming back? There is something about the implacable sea that makes us all children again. We march back down the corridors of our memories, images of long ago flash back, and revelations of friends, sweethearts, young love, Gossamer dreams, first kiss, ephemeral promises, constant laughter, treasured moments, dance in your heart. It was the time of our lives: childhood innocence where we constantly dream and play. After dinner, out on our porch, we watch as the sun extinguishes itself as it gently falls into the sea. A mantle of darkness creeps across the sky and the moon lays down an undulating ribbon of silver. As the sower scatters seeds, so the stars array the heavens. The waves crash on shore and the rippling foam prolongs its song, and fades into a whisper. Sleep comes easily as the repeated resonance of the surf becomes a lullaby, and we say goodbye to another day. We dream of tomorrow which will be even better.

The Innocence of Childhood

Today I wish to write about the little world where children have their existence. Sharing the lives of my children and grandchildren keeps me ever mindful of the innocent wonder of childhood. Do you know that true innocence is ashamed of nothing? When you see children anywhere, when you look into their starry eyes, their sunny faces, and hear their musical laughter, you realize that they possess the one true nobility, virtue. How easy it is to love them. They make you move away from the periphery of your life and reach for your center – their presence erases the signature of sadness – they burgeon the happy side of life's equation. Their hugs release an imprisoned loveliness. You see childhood innocence is incapable of a dark dimension. Neither does it wear hollow badges of dazzling symbols that reek of falsehood. Isn't it strange how we allow only children to intrude into the privacy of our thoughts? In their sleeping faces you will never find discord, betrayal, disorder, discontent, or deceit. In their glowing faces we see the quiet hush of morning, the crimson glory of dawn, the golden sunrise – their lacewing smile beckons the heart to be still. You must be gentle with children – restrain your temper for harsh words bruise the heart of a child. Did you know that the very aged are automatically restored to the innocence of their childhood? And at night when I dream of my grandchildren, I caress the magic lantern. Let me conclude with a few verses from a poem by Father John Shea as he reflects on the "Lord of the Dance."

Now
There was only the morning
And the dancing man of the broken tomb
The story says
He dances still
That is why
Down to this day
We lean over the beds of our babies
And in the seconds before sleep
Tell the story of the undying dancing man
So the dream of Jesus will carry them to dawn.

The Changing Seasons at the Shore

You notice the changes by the many signs ... the absence of haze ... the clearness so stunning that you look beyond the horizon and see tomorrow ... mackerel clouds imbedded in an impeccably blue sky ... the silver glint of the sun on the water's surface ... the sand moist and cool under your feet. The surf can be a noisy thing this time of the year ... but you reflect on an endless roiling ribbon of foamy bubbles ... gulls glide gracefully like children at play ... the slight chill in the wind hastens Summer's retreat, and whispers of Fall's colorful expectations. Here you always feel young ... you relive the downy kisses of yesterday ... the warm handclasp of that girl in the third grade ... the sky reflects the tint of her eyes ... and the breaking waves resound her laughter. You feel a penchant for viewing drifting faces of childhood companions ... travails of young love that might have been ... the skittery times on the playground. A blend of sweet and sad that pulls at your heart and mists your eyes. Diminished by the overpowering vastness of the sea ... in a special moment of awareness ... you ask yourself that profound question, "Am I everything I promised myself to be?" At night a crescent moon hangs low in the sky... the darkness embodies dreams you wish you could have back ... the stars hold their secrets ... but extend their promise to those who conceal their fears. Time for slumber and the surf rumbles her age old lullaby ... sleep comes quickly ... Tinker Bell scatters her magic crystals ... you are a child again safe and warm in the embrace of innocence. Your heart sings musical memories ... all pain is erased ... difficult moments banished ... and all is well in your secret garden.

The Colors of October

"There is something about October that sets the gypsy blood astir." These words from the "Vagabond Song" define the golden month of autumn ... that collage of bright reds, soft yellows, mellow oranges, reserved russets. The beauty catches your breath ... interrupts your thoughts ... signals messages from the past. Always something there to remind you of wistful memories that makes your heart smile ... to retreat into that castle within your soul ... and there to dream in quiet wonder. Did you miss the opportunity to find fulfillment in this dazzling airy grace? Did you lose the chance to find that joy that is the fruit of the spirit? Wait 'til tomorrow we say ... don't you realize that tomorrow may never be yours at all? We engage in a myriad of trivial pursuits ... rushing to nowhere ... frantic scurrying in needless tasks to fill the time ... but end in folly. In reality they become disguised attempts to escape from ourselves ... to run away from what we really are. Take the moment to view the offerings of nature ... run carefree through the golden leaves ... find in its beauty the luster that transforms ... that brings you back to that time in your life where all was full of promise and expectation. The magic slipper would fit ... and you would ride off into the sunset in that golden carriage. Whatever you do, never, ever, ever, shatter the harmony of nature ... to do so is to shatter the harmony of creation. Shame on you if you let it pass. October offers that special moment ... it wishes for you to inherit the peace ... to be the keeper of that golden quiet ... to cradle that lustrous stillness in your heart ... to reap all things good and true ... and to forever dine on the mellow wine of memories.

Winter: A Chilly Disclaimer

We easily forget those portions of winter (January thaw, balmy days) that do not cause us to suffer. What we remember are the winters that put us through our hour of trial. When winter settles in, she becomes brazen and arrogant. She ruefully smiles, then smites us with her harsh vicissitudes. At early morning we shiver, shake, shudder, and stutter. The snow on the ground does not melt. The ice in the driveway does not give way. The ponds, lakes, and river are so frozen you can drive over them. The sun hangs low but gives no warmth. You can chip the brittle sky. And if you throw a stone, the lonesome, vulnerable clouds would shatter. When you venture outside, your nose runs constantly. You don't dare sneeze lest your face crumble. The tips of your fingers and toes pain so that you want to cry. But your resolve will not allow it. This is WINTER, not that imposter of 32 degrees – mud and slush. I rarely ask special favors but you wish the wind would subside to lessen the sting. The new fallen snow is immaculate. You stop, wonder, and wish your soul were as clean. You are so moved that you beseech a special blessing. And in that humble moment you recognize your mortality, and vow to do better to ensure your immortality. You cannot stay out very long. The discomfort brings you to the threshold of malevolence. You step inside and in the warmth of your home you can almost feel the convincing power of the spirit, which you try to apotheosize, but the aura of inscrutability interferes. You prepare a hot cup of tea. And in the rising vapors your thoughts vacillate to earlier times. Out of the catacombs of your soul emerges that innocent, chaste child with waves of golden hair, bayou-blue eyes, and rust-spattered freckles who never was too cold in the winter, never too warm in the summer, never too tired to play, never so exhausted to fail to dream, and never devoid of laughter, energy, spirit, loyalty, warmth, hope, promise, and love. It was a time to be young, and winters were giddy and fun. And every waking moment we passionately pursued friendship and happiness.

The Flowers Bid Farewell

The flowers of summer were prolific. We cut and distributed hundreds of bouquets that warmed many hearts and lifted many spirits. Do you know that the flowers that you give, whatever the occasion, transcribe the message in your heart? To the recipient, the flowers seem to say, "and lend to the rhyme of the poet, the beauty of thy voice". But at the foreboding forecast of Fall's first frost, my dahlias tremble in trepidation. Dahlias are at their peak in the Fall. Multi-colored and sensuous, they are delicate, fragile, and vulnerable. The hard frost comes, and the first glint of sunlight becomes dazzling, reflecting through a myriad of burnished bits of shattered diamonds. And as the rising sun chases the powdery white crystals away, the dahlias take of the color of mourning. Like an avenging angel of the dark, Jack Frost points his icy finger, and beauty and innocence are violated.

There are other flowers in the garden and they respond to Jack Frost differently. The mums play hide and seek. The roses play a game of tag. And the remaining daisies bristle defiantly and will not be intimidated. They will survive to face another day. Even the leaves on the trees die in beauty before succumbing to the call of the ages. But poor, tender winsome dahlias, blackened by the scourge of the cruel forerunner of winter, they fall victim to the solemn ritual of the reaper, and are consigned to eternity.

All seasons have a purpose. And the purpose of melancholy Fall is to remind us that we must die unto ourselves if we are to be regenerated into the warm hope of Spring: that season of mirth, when the warm sun kisses the slumbering earth, and the greening of the land gives promise of a new birth, a new day of resurrection. Spring and flowers give rise to the adage, "beauty is truth, and truth is beauty, that is all you need to know". Fall tells us to bring in the harvest and fill the bins, for cruel Winter approaches.

The Beauty of Autumn

As I ride the countryside, the beauty of Autumn transcends the ability of the human mind to comprehend the wonder of this natural spectacle. The colored foliage of gold, russet, yellow, red, and orange, set amid the evergreen, pulses with nature's sustaining and poetic spirit. The pleasures of every Autumn hang there to be admired, as the warm sun, the splash of colors, fading flowers, make you rummage through the treasure chest of your memories. It becomes easy to succumb to the efficacy of illusion. And yet you hold Autumn to your heart in pure delight. In the gentle rustle of the multi-tinted leaves of Fall, I see the face of that girl in the third grade … a soft wind whispers her name … I hear her lilting laughter … I remember how easily love comes at that age … and how quickly and painfully it can end. Do you know our greatest need is boundless love? That true love heals the many mindless scars of life? This feeling manifests itself most when you hug your grandchildren, and hear their unencumbered laughter, their excited recitation of yesterday's simple events, and their warm little hands in yours as you take a walk. It is the grandchildren who teach us to use this wonderful season to forge a permanent fondness for each other that nothing could ever destroy. The door of winter is opening. And with it comes the chill and hard frost that blemishes the flowers, tarnishes the fields, and makes naked the trees. But if you remain faithful to the breaking of the bread, then there is no ill wind, no frigid measure, and no spurious frost that can ever sully the blossoms in your heart.

The Music in Our Lives

The music in our lives evokes many emotions. The rhythm, lyrics, melodies ... we all have our favorites ... and when we hear them, we recall the moments that were special and indelible. The older we get, the deeper and more lasting these moments become. Let me pass unto you those songs and melodies that cause me to imagine new worlds ... invent new experiences that haunt me still. Whenever Perry Como sings, "No Other Love Have I" or "'Til the End of Time", a gentle hand strokes my heart ... and the great love of my life in apparition floats by ... the wonder ... the wild desire ... the saved up wishes ... the inexpressible charm ... enkindle the cozy fire of affection ... and I drink the nectar from the jeweled cup. And when Roger Whittaker comes forth with, "The Wind Beneath My Wings", ... the cosmic resonance of our children's singing eyes drift by in a deep blue cloudless sky. What is the music in your life, where you need to marshal the forces to fight back the tears? Other songs give rise to other emotions. You can sense the despair as Neil Diamond sings these words from "I Am...I Said" "I'm lost and I don't even know why", or "Find me walking that long, long road". You can feel the heartbreak of love lost as Nat King Cole renders, "A Petal Fell", or Anne Murray's, "I'm so lonesome I can cry". These are disturbing lyrics by Perry Como from his "Impossible". "I would sell my very soul and not regret it", and warm nostalgia in words from Neil Diamond's, "Some things will never change like saying I love you". You see, we are all scarred by life's encounters ... but the edifying, spirit lifting efficacy of our music, keeps us full of hope and dreams ... it keeps inviolable the human spirit. The music in our lives enables us to explore possibilities the world says do not exist.

The Mystique of Colorado Springs

The plane touches down gently. Through the windows we see the snow covered mountains. The scene rekindles the love deep inside. At the Olympic Training Center we have an unobstructed view of Pike's Peak; the tallest, most majestic mountain in this range. This monarch rises so high, that on most mornings, its head is hidden, sleeping in the clouds. When the sun breaks through and the snow-capped peak is freed, the sight commands your obeisance. Here is where our most gifted and talented athletes train for Olympic competition. The facilities are state-of-art, and everyone friendly, courteous, helpful. We visit the Air Force Academy and are enthralled by the beauty. Because of the elevation, exhaustion comes easily, even during mild exertion. Deer, eagles, and falcons summon your respect as they wander and maneuver freely. The gem at the Academy is the Chapel. Silver spires interlaced with stained glass, sparkle and shimmer in the bright sunlight. The weather is cold, and as you stand inside and gaze at the wonder, you fear to make a sound, lest the glass, like icicles, shatters. We move slowly, silently, afraid to disturb the reverence that envelops us. In this setting, at this moment, all doubters become believers. Because God is here. You feel His presence. Close your eyes, and in the depth of your imploration, you feel His embrace. Do you know that the closer you move toward God, the more unworthy you feel, and the more fearful you become? We visit Broadmoor and briefly taste the extravagance of the privileged. At the famous ice-skating rink nearby, we observe Olympic hopefuls of all ages practicing routines just as Dorothy Hamill, Debbie Thomas, and Jill Trenary before them. On our departure, the plane slowly rises, and we are lost in the mysticism of the mountains. Somewhere inside your mind, the Chapel flashes clear and solemn. Glistening spires reach for the heavens, you are haunted by the eternal silence of that infinite space, holy, sacred, divine. In our pilgrimage through life, our soul longs for the beauty of the abstract, the transcendental. If you do not find it in Colorado Springs, then you never shall.

The Star of Christmas

I get sentimental and nostalgic at Christmas, don't you? Especially when I muse upon the times of my children and grandchildren. And my eyes get misty when I dream of my own childhood of distant yesterdays. Central to me are the Christ Star, the babe of Bethlehem, and the innocence of children the babe signifies. In the holy hush of the cold night of Christmas Eve, overhead the sanctities of the stars shine forevermore. And one really stands out. It twinkles, and sparkles and glistens, and shimmers, bigger and brighter than all of the rest. It reflects the eternal splendors of the heavens, and the stillness causes you to hold your breath - your heart grows light. Do you know that we are all guided by that star? On Christmas Eve, when all is quiet, step out into the night and scan the Eastern sky. When you find it, then you will understand. Listen to what Merrit Malloy says: "It is only when we are in love or when we're little that Christmas really comes true ... in between it can break your heart with expectation." And Charles Dickens writes, "It is good to be children sometimes, and never better than at Christmas time." There is never a time so beautiful, for children, for you, and for me. You see the Christmas mystery is embodied in its many symbols of love. It is a gentle time of peace and serenity. Christmas is timeless. And wouldn't it be wonderful if the whole year through we kept Christmas in our hearts? Do you know why, on the night, I sleep with an inerasable smile? It is the little feet of my grandchildren dancing gently on my heart.

The Melancholy Season – Winter

William Cullen Bryant writes, "The melancholy days are come, the saddest of the year, of wailing winds and naked woods and meadows brown and sere". He writes of the short days of winter … the frigid hush that lie over everything … the long voice of the chill wind that howls a dreary wail. Even a smile comes begrudgingly. The ache in your hip … the twinge in your back … the stiffness in your knee … the crick in your neck … small discomforts that dissipate in the warmth of summer, nag on and on in Winter's grip. The carefree gait of Spring is forgotten … and you walk the lumber of the aged, surefooted and slow under ice and snow. Your breath is visible … your teeth chatter … bundled and trundled, you wonder how people make love in the Arctic. And yet winters were fun when you were young, remember? It was the majesty of new fallen snow … the glistening ice on the pond … icicles that draped the eaves … and the urge to throw that first snowball. The weeping gloom of winter can rob you of heart and hope … and more than in any other season, we fear the sound of being alone. We frantically engage in that restless searching for the calm Easter wind. In the warmth of Spring, it is easy to fill yourself with an abundance of love and share it with everyone. And yet Winter offers plentiful opportunities to be open to each moment … to spend time with yourself in the quiet of your heart … to listen to the still voices of yesterday … to recall pleasures of special moments … and to nestle safe and content in the warmth of that peace. It is strange, but we find our happiest moments in unexpected places … even in unwelcome winter.

The New Year

Another calendar falls into history, and the new, shiny page of 1991 boldly stares you down. Yes, we are all slowly growing older. Does that frighten you? Thoughts emerge from the mists of time and remind us of our journey through the long eternity of yesterday. Fear not. For you see the nobility of growing old is measured by your ability to survive your reputation. Although history is a harsh judge, it rarely denies you the pleasures of the past you enjoy in fantasy – especially in your childhood. Don't you know that you are part of all that was, all that is, and all that will be? That is the wisdom of our time. And by what standards do you measure yourself? It is not the number of years gone by, but the trail of goodness you leave behind … the smiles, the laughter, the comfort, the good feelings, the worth, the love, the reassurances … that crisp collage of kindness, caring, and concern that you leave in your wake. These are the milestones that give meaning and substance to your life. For many of us, sometimes our whole life is defined by one special moment in history. That is why, for all of us, there is this compelling need to support the standards of civility toward each other. We need to uphold the principle of consistent application of decency and courtesy in our mutual behavior. If you wish to make time your ally, then never breach the boundaries of friendship. Consign your deeds to the comfort and peace of all whose lives you touch. In the time ahead, extract the goodness of yourself from the inside out. And whatever you do, never, never, never, become a termagant. In their sour disposition and incessant railing, they constantly usurp your precious time, and abscond with bits of your life.

The Samaritan in All of Us

Sitting here musing about our demise of the "Moral Midnight" so eloquently phrased by John Cardinal O'Connor, I feel the need to preach. You see all good writing contains the elements of teaching and preaching. If you will allow me, I will produce a short missive, using the parable of the Good Samaritan as our foundation. There lies within all of us a Good Samaritan. Only we keep him/her imprisoned. We do not release him/her as frequently as we should. I am sure you will agree with that. Do you know that it is sinful to deny the calling of your true self? To disregard the beckoning of Lady Wisdom? To set a course that chafes from misdirection? To let injustice prevail due to your non-involvement? To close your eyes to cruelty? I wonder at the millennium of human suffering that could have been avoided had the good people of the world acted accordingly. I marvel at the giants of humanitarian service – the Sister Theresa's, the Doctor Dooley's, the Father Damien's, the Gandhi's of the world. They were marked with a special sign, dedicated to the eradication of injustice and inhumanity. How many times have you asked yourself: What can I do? How can I help? What is my calling? To make a difference you do not have to slay a dragon; donate large sums to charity; build a children's hospital; find a cure for cancer; become president; develop an energy source that is inexpensive. All of us, in our daily pursuits, can fulfill the promise, by a little kindness, a word, a touch, a smile, a gesture, a look, to those in our charge, those near us. All about us are people who need something from us. But too often we interpose barriers between ourselves and them. Never let yourself become so busy, so pre-occupied, that you subjugate the Samaritan in yourself. When the occasion arises, let the Samaritan come forth, freely and volitionally. Put the sun in your voice, the music in your eyes, and the love in your touch. You will find that it will "make your day". You see the fundamental priority of kindness never changes.

The Sights and Sounds
of a Trying Winter

The predominant sound of a trying winter I remember most is the rumble of snow plows at night ... the ugly, grimy, mounds along the roadside ... made pristine with each new snowfall, then sullied again. The ice encrusted auto and the arduous scraping ... the stormy days and howling wind ... lashing rain and driving snow ... pelting sleet ... whipping branches ... rattling windows. Do you know that the wind has a voice of its own? How can you forget the unrelenting cold and foreboding ice? Did you ever see the squirrel searching for food in deep snow? He burrows and rises and burrows again ... seemingly enjoying himself immensely. The birds cluster in the forsythia bushes and wait for me to scatter feed ... the gulls, crows, and a lone goose come and wreak havoc. The blue jays are the strangest of all ... they dive, pick up a morsel, and flutter away. A pair of wild doves sit beneath my neighbor's feeder and wait for seeds to fall. Did you ever try to decipher the raucous cry of a bantering crow? Patches of lawn are beginning to show as snow and ice retreat before a warming sun. Sections of garden are clearing ... tulip and daffodil shoots are breaking the surface ... crocuses have risen but have not yet blossomed. Tree buds are emerging ... a sure sign that Spring will soon follow. Do you know when cruelty is incurred, wild are the surges that break over the soul? Winter is that season that can stultify our disposition ... make our responses as chilly as the weather. But I say, seek the peaceful haven of Spring ... counter rudeness with courtesy ... gather each day unto your arms and flee the tempest of daily struggles ... recite the winged words of poetry ... and cherish the sweet moments that live in your heart.

The True Spirit of Giving

The spirit of Christmas is never really out of season. And this past Christmas has concluded the most prolific period of giving we will experience the remainder of this year. The outpouring of gifts will not be matched until the calendar again comes up for renewal. You see, we often reveal ourselves by our gifts. And yet we gather nothing when we give out of duty, expectation, or favor. Listen to what the sages say about giving: "The only gift is a portion of thyself". (Emerson) "Rich gifts wax poor, when the giver proves unkind." (Shakespeare, Hamlet) We should give with propriety and grace ... to fulfill the needs of others ... never expecting a return. Lavishness is not generosity. Neither are the gifts of seduction. Perfunctory giving is the hypocrisy of being someone you really do not wish to be ... it ravages the very substance of your soul. It has been said that he who gives his heart, will not deny his money. Do you find yourself here? You see we enkindle hope by compassionate giving to those in need. The spirit of Christmas is born of giving, and the best gift you can give is yourself ... the priceless charm of a warm smile ... an understanding look ... an affectionate hand clasp ... a consoling hug ... a friendly touch of a shoulder ... a loving kiss ... tender feelings that make you want to touch the heart of others. These are the true and abiding gifts of Christmas ... the true spirit of giving.

What Did You Do New Years Eve?

When asked the above question, most people do not have trouble remembering. We never seem to forget where we were, whom we were with, and what we were doing on any New Years Eve in the past. By the same token, there are some eves you would like to forget. Like the time you chug-a-lugged a bottle of champagne and had to wait until next year to sing "Auld Lang Syne". Or the time you imbibed too much and needed to be rescued when the dance floor started spinning, and you thought it was an earthquake.

New Years eves have been good to me. When you understand that the transition from one year to the next is supposed to be a dedication to change for the better in your life. You are supposed to leave your bad habits, your bad tendencies, your bad disposition, behind with the old calendar. And as the sun rises on the new year, you promise your life will take on new meaning, new direction, new purpose, new resolution. You promise everyone a kinder and gentler tomorrow. But does it happen?????
Sometimes!!!!!

Together, let's take inventory of our past New Year's Eves, and try to remember them chronologically and whimsically:

1. The Wackiest - 1935 (10 years old) – being awakened by the noise when a fox got into the chicken coop.
2. The Saddest – 1941 (15 years old) – right after Pearl Harbor – older brothers (5) joining Army and Navy.
3. Most Frustrating – 1942 (16 years old) – being stood up – girl's father would not let her go to the YMCA dance.
4. Most Unforgettable – 1943-44 (18, 19 years old) in U.S. Navy in South Pacific and Philippines at sea, standing watch – war as usual.
5. 1945 (20 years old) – St. Albans Naval Hospital.
6. The Wildest – 1946 (21 years old) – out of service (Hooray) – with friends, crashed house party – thrown out for hell raising – returned with hammer and nails and nailed front door shut.

7. Most Memorable – 1949 (my age henceforth will not be recorded) at party, chased all night by a young sculptress – wanted me to sit for her – claimed I reminded her of Julius Caesar because of my Roman Nose.

8. Most Hilarious – 1951 – on way home early morning with friends – dog started barking because our singing disturbed him – we set fire to his dog house – owner came out screaming – we told him fire started when a shooting star hit the dog house – he believed us.

9. The Happiest – 1955 – became engaged to Carol on Christmas Day – still celebrating on New Year's Eve.

10. Most Fun – 1956 – out with friends – men dropping ice cubes down bodice of women – women getting even by dropping cubes down our pants.

11. Most Endearing – 1957 – first son, Peter ("Casey") born – coming home seeing him asleep so peacefully.

12. Most Poignant - 1965 - early morning, coming home checking on children (4) Peter, Tom, Cathy, Charlie - in bed with all of their Christmas toys.

13. Most Resigned – 1980 to present – at home with Guy Lombardo on T.V. - watching crowd at Times Square – champagne toast – in bed at 12:30.

Look back, try remembering yours, and let's compare stories.

Valentines Day –
A Celebration of Love

Valentines Day has passed, and the cards we sent to those we love …
cards filled with rhyme and poetry … words that define our tender
and fragile feelings … have been discarded and forgotten. Valentines
Day, a celebration of love, is it a one day occasion? I think not. True
love is eternal and enduring. Love means being at ease with others in
silence. "My soul for quiet seeks", St. Paul reminds us. In your solitude
take time to listen … immerse yourself in that vast forever of golden
quiet, where in the stillness you will hear the music of the stars. You
must let go the small resentments that clutter your mind and sap your
energy. Fill yourself with tender feelings that make you want to touch
the face of others. When you recite the sweet words of love in prose,
you set another's heart aglow … they are the sunbeams that play on
the ocean. Be not troubled by mournful yesterdays or the kiss you
never had. Bring hope to those you serve by kind words and deeds …
to help them find their place in the sun. Be kind with your gifts of
heart and mind … share your harvest and fortune of your goodness. I
say woe to those who have no peace to give. Never, ever, ever, let cold
disregard, indifference, become that icy cave … the burial site of your
love, compassion, affection. Do you know why so many individuals are
unable to accept love? Perhaps they feel they can never fully comply with
loves demands. After all, if they give themselves over to these demands,
what will they have left for themselves? Therefore to celebrate Valentines
Day once a year is enough for them. If you are to open the gates of your
secret prison … and set yourself free … then celebrate Valentines Day
every day.

The Wonder of Spring

Andrew Greeley writes: "Perhaps the worst thing which can happen to us humans, is to lose our wonder. The tragedy of closing your mind and heart to the wonders of Spring ... the wonder of a new born baby ... the wonder of love ... the wonder of Christmas ... the wonder and glory of sunrise and sunset ... the wonder of new fallen snow." Only fools and the hard-hearted disengage their feelings from this magnificent season, when flowers bloom and robins sing. You need to appreciate the surface to understand the depth. Do you know that stolen kisses are sweetest in Spring? Spring is more that just a season ... it is a time when snow melts away ... and the daffodils and tulips wash away the scars of winter. It is a time when that girl in the third grade haunts me most ... in her voice I hear the warmth of Spring ... her laughter makes the flowers grow ... in her eyes the sunlight of innocence dances ... in her hands, the flush of first love ... and I feel her touch still. Unless you learn to cherish the beauty of Spring, you will never be free from your poverty of aesthetic appreciation. More than ever, now is the time to expunge yourself of negative thoughts and actions ... they can be so destructive. And never, ever, ever lose your capacity of wonder and hope ... and never stop saying "I love you."

True Friendship

I search the dynamics of human behavior, but nowhere can I find a formula, an explanation, a diagnosis for true friendship. Do you know why? Because true friendship is a covenant … a profound bond between two people that decrees loyalty and love … qualities that will not languish with distress. It is not a queasy thing that withers upon confrontation. Friendship displays a durability that withstands the test of time. Emerson writes, "To have a friend, you must be a friend." True friends cry and celebrate together. In trying circumstances, you need not call a friend, they call you. True friends do not engage in perfumed and gallant words … for these are not kin to sincerity. Adlai Stevenson once said, "Flattery is all right, if you do not inhale." Do you know that prosperity makes friends, but adversity tries them? Cicero says it better, "The shift of fortune tests the reliability of friends." Treasure the laughter and love of true friends … it responds from the heart … it stands firm … it remains constant … and endures. Friendship is born of struggle and hope. Many marriages go wrong because man and wife cease being good friends. Aristotle defines it best, "Friendship is a single soul dwelling in two bodies." How many true friends do you have? Can you name them? And lastly from the Good Book: "Be fond of a friend and keep faith with them." Sirach 27:17. "A faithful friend is beyond price." Sirach 5:16.

Wave Summer Goodbye

We are at the shore again to catch the transformation of summer into autumn. The billowy clouds with their dark edges are cold looking and drift low in the sky. The muted sun glitters off the rippling ocean surface, and reflects a million bright and smiling faces of innocent children. A few solitary figures dot the long stretches of empty beach but you do not give way to loneliness. In fact you cherish the solitude, the quiet time, to be alone with your thoughts. The chill wind swirls the sand in small circles and seems to be waving goodbye to summer. The surf sings the song of somnolence as it rushes ashore and retreats in wakes of sizzling bubbles. With no humidity, your vision is unlimited. And as you gaze across the elongated elegance of the horizon you are awed by the immensity of the ocean … you are dwarfed by the incomprehensible magnitude … you want to walk beyond the sunset, beyond time, beyond limitation. Every one of us, enjoys in fantasy, the pleasures of the past, especially our childhood. So whenever I am at the side of the sea, I have this irrational urge to go back to that time … perhaps I invest too much of myself. Nevertheless, I am haunted by the face of that girl in the third grade … the soft surf murmurs her name … I bask in the dusky glow of her glistening blue eyes … those pleasant, sigh evoking memories come to visit … and when I reach for her hand, I am awakened by the sounds of today. Isn't it strange how we shape our lives by the experiences we have had? Night quickly creeps in like a silent marauder. The sky takes on the aura of theater as tiny fluorescent stars dance and twinkle. It is here that love and hope and promise perches in your soul and gives your spirit wings. And when you finally close your eyes for the night, sleep will not come unless you allow the whispering surf to tell you its secrets.

When Does the First Firefly
of Summer Appear?

I saw my first firefly of the summer on June 18th. It was growing dark and I was surprised by his appearance. He was all alone which surprised me even more. Nobody notices fireflies anymore. In our busy-ness they don't seem to evoke the same delight that they did when we were young. As children, they were so abundant, that we would fill jars with them, and carry them around as lanterns. It seems many of Summer's pleasant sights are hard to find … butterflies … red wing blackbirds alighting on cattails … wild canaries skittering on sunflowers … kingfishers and ospreys in their frenzied dives … wild grapes, raspberries, blackberries, blueberries. Where have they gone? These memories for me never age. Memories of stardust and moonbeams on River Salmon … wishes and dreams play hide and seek … and you are overwhelmed in that quiet, calm enchantment, in the silence of a summer evening … the rhythm of the ocean where sea and sand and sky pulsate eternity. Have you ever hung your heart on a summer star? And summer teaches us the ultimate wisdom … that truth is absolute. What fools we are as we race about in undisciplined frenzy of petty ambition. Summer is the time for quiet interludes … to fill yourself with moments of truth and beauty and sudden delight … this is what brings peace and tranquility … embrace it and say no more.

Time to go Home ...
Home to the River

Everyone should have a river in their life ... a river to go home to ... to gather the collective moments of your life ... to find the lost dimension of yourself ... to join that part of your life that we have become, to that part that stayed behind. It was Lady Wisdom beckoned me to the river ... and love called my name. It was on River Salmon ... in a summer season ... when soft was the sun ... that I met the love of my life. We courted by canoe ... in warm sunny days ... enchanting moonlight ... star-filled nights ... cool evening breezes ... and always the river saying, "hush" ... for when true love is deep, words are never necessary. We go back home ... home to the river to reclaim the dreams, desires, attachments, and memories that formed the substance of our being ... and to which we cling, and embrace, and long for, affectionately. The river leaves an indelible mark on your soul ... a constant calling to return and retrieve those pleasant memories that stir the emulsion of happiness ... to reconcile the omissions with the deeds of our life. Colorful sunsets touched and stirred our love to forge an eternal bonding. Shooting stars would inscribe our names across the sky, then fall to earth in silvery crystals. Come with me and ride that dream back to the stream ... where water lilies beamed ... and hummingbirds beat a lullaby on invisible wings ... where the night holds a melody of its own ... the soft mist bridges a fundamental truth ... when two hearts touch, life becomes a rapture of truth and beauty and repose and never ending delight. In reverie we all go back in time and rekindle our happiest moments ... to again embrace the perfection of passion and excitement of first love in summer ... that lurked, alluring and enticing where the gentle waters flow. The river holds many secrets. And speaks only to those who remain faithful to her. You see, love and friendship are never for sale ... not are they ever open to deceit or compromise. Like the river, their course is steady and true ... and full of dreams, promises, and quiet expectations that circumscribe the dimension of peace.

The single best augury is to fight for your country in a noble cause.

-The Ancient Greeks

John P. Gawlak was the youngest of five brothers to serve in WWII. He joined the Navy at the age of 17 and served in the South Pacific (1943-46) aboard the U.S.S. Whitney. His ship was cited with a Letter of Commendation by Admiral William "Bull" Halsey, Commander of the 7th Fleet.

Lt. Carol Hart Stanley U.S. Army - Served during the Korean War (1953-56), as an Occupational Therapist at Walter Reed Army Medical Center in Washington D.C. and at Brooke Army Hospital, Ft. Sam Houston, San Antonio, Texas.

Note: It was a difficult courtship. Being a former enlisted man, I had to salute my future wife before I could kiss her.